Iran

T0165135

Polity Histories series

Iran

Ali M. Ansari

polity

First published in 2024 by Polity Press

Polity Press
65 Bridge Street
Cambridge CB2 1UR, UK

Polity Press
111 River Street
Hoboken, NJ 07030, USA

ISBN-13: 978-1-5095-4150-8
ISBN-13: 978-1-5095-4151-5 (pb)

A catalogue record for this book is available from the British Library.

Library of Congress Control Number: 2023938502

Typeset in 11 on 13 Berkeley by
Cheshire Typesetting Ltd, Cuddington, Cheshire
Printed and bound in the UK by CPI Group (UK) Ltd, Croydon

For further information on Polity, visit our website:
politybooks.com

For Mimi

Contents

Map of Iran

Acknowledgements

All books are collective efforts and this one is no exception. I am grateful to my two anonymous reviewers for their careful reading of the text and comments, and to my copy-editor, Leigh Mueller, for diligently reviewing the text and ironing out the inevitable incoherencies that emerge. I am also grateful to the National Archive for permission to use extracts from their files. Above all, I would like to thank my editor, Louise Knight, and Inès Boxman, who piloted this particular ship safely to port. Any remaining errors or infelicitous use of language are mine and mine alone.

Introduction
A Revolutionary Land

Iran has rarely been out of the news, but rarely in it for positive reasons. Indeed, for much of the history of the Islamic Republic, Iran's relationship with the outside world has been beset by a series of crises, not least the 'Islamic' revolution of 1979 itself – perhaps the first televised revolution in history – which painted a brutal and bloody picture of the unfolding developments. The US Embassy hostage crisis, which was broadcast nightly on US television, ensured that developments in Iran were seared into an increasingly unforgiving American mind.

Since then, each decade has been marked by a particular crisis: the war against Iraq shaped much of the 1980s, followed by the confrontation over the Rushdie fatwa which coloured relations over the 1990s, and then in the aftermath of 9/11 the seemingly insoluble crisis over Iran's nuclear programme. These crises have in many ways defined the way in which the West has seen Iran, and have also served to cloud our perspective and disguise the domestic political drivers that have shaped the country.

Nothing shows this better than the general surprise at the latest turn of events in September 2022 following the death in custody of Mahsa Jina Amini, at the hands of the Morality Police. The subsequent uprising, led by women, in pursuit of basic rights, can only be understood and appreciated in the context of the general deterioration of State–society relations in the Islamic Republic over the last two decades.

But, more strikingly, the recent protests echo and reflect the drive towards constitutionalism and fundamental rights which has been at the heart of Iranian political history for more than a century, beginning with the launch of Iran's first revolution, the Constitutional Revolution of 1906. Largely overshadowed by the Islamic Revolution in 1979, this earlier revolution has arguably had a much more profound impact on political ideas and activism; it is a lode stone and reference point for all students of Iranian politics.

The importance of a constitution and the rule of law, a means to regulate relations between State and society within an Iranian framework, continues to energize politics in Iran to this day, and however much governing elites seek to suppress or eradicate these ideas, they stubbornly resurface with each generation.

It is, as such, important for the reader to appreciate just how ingrained and embedded these ideas are, how they have been integrated into the fabric of Iranian politics over the last two centuries and why, as a result, they are not going away. Many of the themes that have shaped Iranian history and politics to this day have been long in gestation and took form in the years leading to and including the Constitutional

Revolution. These years provide the template on which all other matters rest, giving shape to the ideas and tensions which occupy Iranians to this day.

The dominating theme has been how to contend with the challenge posed by the West, and modernity in general. How, to put it in simple terms, could Iran be returned to the Great Power status that many Iranians felt was her birth right.

At the beginning of the nineteenth century, Iran – or Persia in the Western vernacular – identified as an empire: not just any empire, but the oldest and most esteemed of all empires, which had perhaps seen better days but whose history suggested that better days would return. Even in the twilight of the Safavid Empire (1501–1722) when its imperial pretensions were real, as the Huguenot Sir John Chardin noted caustically, they continued to enjoy grandiose notions of their imperial authority.[1]

By the turn of the nineteenth century, even with the further retreat of borders, that imperial mentality remained stubborn and immovable. Tradition – and imperial mythology – told Iranians that not only was their dominion the oldest in the world, but it was moreover the centre of the universe and the best of earthly territories. Indeed, the founder of the new Qajar dynasty (1797–1925) had 'acquiesced' to the royal diadem as long as his new subjects accepted his determination to restore Iran to its rightful greatness.

Identified as a 'crossroads of civilization', Iran occupied a plateau in south-west Asia on the 'silk road' connecting the West with China. Bounded by the Caspian Sea to the north and the Persian Gulf to the south, the much-diminished imperium was still by the nineteenth century a large country possessed of diverse climes, shielded on two sides by two extensive mountain ranges – the Zagros to the west and the Alborz to the north – the arid climate of its core contrasting with the lush forests of the Caspian seaboard. To the south-west, the plateau descended into the Mesopotamian plain where the Shatt al-Arab waterway – the confluence of the Euphrates and Tigris rivers – demarcated the border with the Ottoman Empire (and latterly Iraq).

Even before oil, gas and other minerals were discovered in substantial quantities in the twentieth century, European statesmen were acutely aware of the geopolitical significance of the area. In Lord Curzon's memorable, if somewhat romanticized, view: 'Turkestan, Afghanistan, Transcaspia, Persia – to many these names breathe only a sense of utter remoteness or a memory of strange vicissitudes and of moribund romance. To me, I confess, they are the pieces on a chessboard upon which is being played out a game for the dominion of the world.'[2]

The Challenge of the West

The arrival of the Europeans in the shape of both the Russian and British Empires quickly served notice that an imperial resurgence would not automatically follow, as night followed day. Instead, the European challenge was of an altogether different nature. They may be curious about the 'Persians', aware about them from the religious and classical texts, and they might have been seduced by the cultural richness they encountered, but they were driven by new ideas of civilization and progress and were more than sufficiently confident to deal with the ancient empire of the Persians.

More to the point, as the Russians were to show in two devastating wars (1804–13 and 1826–8), this new Europe had found a way to wage war that the Iranians found difficult to contend with. It was not so much that the Iranians were lacking in bravery, but there were new systems of warfare being deployed that only modern states, with better forms of administration, could sustain.

Iranian reformers of the nineteenth century soon realized that this was not a matter of tinkering at the edges. Modern armies could not be procured and sustained with the old methods; new approaches would be required in both politics and economy. But how best to start the process of 'modernization'? Could one catalyse change through economic reform or was it better to grasp the nettle through political reform?

British observers were in little doubt about the nature of the problem faced by the Iranians. Drawing on their own experience over the previous two centuries, they argued, with considerable force, that the problem faced by Iranians was neither sociological

nor, as some would later argue, biological, but political. This could be rectified by applying discipline,
expanding education and enforcing the rule of law.

The idea that Iran's ills could be addressed through
the application of different – better – methods was
enthusiastically endorsed by Iranian reformers, who
drank copiously from the well of Enlightenment
Whiggism, digesting the wonders of British industrialization and progress, and pondering on the secrets
of liberty. British ideas were especially pervasive in
the post-Napoleonic period, when the ideas of the
French Revolution, never far from the surface as far
as state building was concerned, were nevertheless
considered inappropriate for a country that sought to
retain its religion and monarchy, albeit under different
management.

The Challenge of Reform

The debate on how reform should be managed, however, remained and tended to oscillate between those
who emphasized political or economic-led reform
and those who preferred some combination of both.
In the first decades of the nineteenth century, Iranian
statesmen had focused on the reform of the army but
accepted that a more fundamental reform of the State
and its administration would be required. How this
might be achieved in the face of stubborn resistance
from what may be loosely described as the 'forces of
reaction' – principally the monarch – was another

matter, where indolence and inertia appeared to rule the day.

As Mohammad Shah lay dying in 1848, his minister consoled him by noting that he left a stable country devoid of the sort of revolution then gripping much of Europe. Nothing could have been further from the truth. Venality and corruption had infected the body politic, money was perennially short and, to make matters worse, the country faced a religious insurrection known as the Babi Revolt, after Ali Mohammad Shirazi – known as the Bab (the gate) – proclaimed himself the Mahdi, the twelfth Imam of the Shias, returned at the end of time to inaugurate a new era.

Iran had been a Shia Muslim state since the Safavids imposed the minority branch of Islam on their subjects from the sixteenth century. It helped to distinguish the Safavids from their Ottoman rivals, but it also provided for other distinctions as far as domestic politics was concerned. Twelver Shi'ism was distinguished by a belief in the hereditary succession of the Muslim community through the Prophet's family and his son-in-law Ali, the first of the twelve Imams, along with the belief that the Imams could interpret the law, a privilege which in their absence could be practised by 'chosen' intermediaries and religious jurists (clerics). In this case, the Bab had declared himself the twelfth Imam, returned along with the abrogation of all religious law, leading dramatically to the first public unveiling of a woman by one of his disciples Tahereh.

The revolt, which was suppressed with some brutality (the Bab himself was executed), shattered the prevailing religious orthodoxies and encouraged people to think the unthinkable. Others who were appalled by both the emergence and treatment of a millenarian movement were further convinced of the necessity of reform. The Babi Revolt would in time give birth to a new faith, that of the Bahais.

Political volatility was followed in 1857 by defeat to Britain, in the one – and, to date, only – Anglo-Persian War. Britain subjected Iran to much more modest terms than the Treaty of Turkmenchai (1828) which had ended the wars with Russia, thereby winning the peace as emphatically as it had won the war. Iranian statesmen then decided that a better route to success might be economic – and indirect – rather than overtly political, a position that British interlocutors increasingly accepted, not least because they would be the principle beneficiaries of this new approach.

It proved to be highly controversial, not least because the Russians were not keen on allowing the British to acquire economic interests at their expense. Some concessions, like that for the new telegraph network, were pursued because they serviced India, but others were pursued by private interests keen to profit from a country largely untouched by economic development. They benefitted from Iranian short-termism and lack of experience in negotiations, leading to contracts that often embarrassed the British Foreign Office, such was the largesse on offer.

Indeed, the Reuter Concession of 1872 was so notorious that Curzon described it as 'the most complete
and extraordinary surrender of the entire industrial
resources of a kingdom into foreign hands that has
probably ever been dreamed of, much less accom-
plished in history'.[3]

It was soon cancelled, but Reuter was later com-
pensated by being awarded the right to establish the
first bank in Iran, with full rights to issue notes. The
British Imperial Bank of Persia effectively served as
Iran's central bank until the rule of Reza Shah. If the
concessions did help to catalyse reform, they did so
primarily by exposing the venality of the Qajar State,
most obviously in the person of the monarch whose
interest in reform appeared limited to the amount of
money he could extract in short order from conces-
sionaires. One especially tawdry concession, giving a
monopoly on all tobacco sales to a British entrepreneur,
proved to be the straw that broke the camel's back,
and an alliance of clergy, intellectuals and merchants
forced its cancellation through a nationwide Tobacco
Boycott (1891). This alliance, which witnessed the
first 'political' application of a fatwa (religious ruling),
was a signpost of things to come.

A Revolution of the Mind?

If the means by which reform might be implemented
continued to be debated, there was little doubt that
Iranians needed a revolution of the mind that moved

them from being selfish subjects to selfless citizens of
a reinvigorated nation – an imperial nation rooted in
history, but a nation nonetheless with a clear sense of
itself and a pride, but not conceit, in its past.

The only way to reconcile tradition and modernity, argued Iran's reformers, was to be rooted and
to have a clear sense of where one had come from.
Was this primarily Iranian, or Islamic, or indeed a
combination of both? Most appreciated that the construction of the 'nation' could only proceed and reach
a successful conclusion if Iranians understood the
cosmopolitan nature of their inheritance, founded in
a shared history and language for which Providence
had provided them with the perfect repository: a
poetic epic, redacted by the eleventh century, known
as the *Book of Kings* (*Shahnameh*). This epic contained
the history, myths and legends of the Iranians from
the moment of Creation till the fall of the last great
Persian empires to the Arab Muslims in the seventh
century AD. This shared literary-historical inheritance bound the Persianate world but was of especial
value to the inhabitants of Iran, the political heirs
of the epic, and Iran's early nationalists understood
its power and utility in helping to shape and bind a
modern identity.

This was not an identity shorn of religion, but it
was one shorn of superstition. Drawing on the ideas
of the anglophone Enlightenment in particular, religion was not regarded as antithetical to progress, but
early thinkers followed broadly secular models which

dictated that 'Church' and 'State' should be held separate. This was as much to protect the purity of religion as it was to desacralize the State, and it is remarkable that the experience of the Islamic Republic, where religion was once again injected into the body politic, has again encouraged thinkers to revert to the secular distinction. The Islamic Revolution, they argued had intended to provide a moral guide for politics, but instead it had resulted in the politicization – and corruption – of religion.

All these debates and tensions were laid bare during the constitutional period and continue to reverberate to this day, with one distinct difference. One of the reasons the Constitutional Revolution faltered was because the politically conscious and active parts of society were limited. Iran did not enter the twentieth century with a print culture of any significance. Literacy was low. But, through the twentieth century, the social fabric of the country changed, becoming better educated, better connected and more aware. The country began the complex process of modernization and industrialization.

Society, which had enjoyed a cultural cohesion, now increasingly enjoyed a political cohesion and unity of purpose. Where the Persian language had been the primary language of perhaps half the population, technology and education now ensured it was both standardized and understood throughout the country. Technology at once allowed the centralization and diffusion of power. It empowered the modern state, but new means of communication soon served to empower society too, building links within the country but also extending outwards.

By the end of the twentieth century, Iranians found themselves increasingly connected to a global community, not least facilitated by an extensive diaspora that had emerged after the Islamic Revolution. This global community further reinforced the impulse for change and, if intellectuals had been affected in the nineteenth century, now ideas were penetrating on a societal scale. The balance of power between State and society was beginning to change and much of what we see on the streets of Iran today is a reflection of that changing dynamic.

Approach and Argument

This short history seeks to distil those 'essential' aspects of the development of Iran over the last two centuries which can best provide the general reader with a critical appreciation and understanding of why we are where we are. It is by its very nature an abridgement and there is much detail that has been left out. It is, as a consequence, a more argumentative piece. But those whose interest has been piqued may wish for a deeper dive by perusing some of the material listed in the brief guide to further reading.

The text, as well as being an abridgement, has deliberately avoided the liberal use of referencing or the use of Persian terms. This has not always been possible, but, for example, I have tended to refer to 'parliament' throughout rather than 'Majles'. Where Persian words have been used, I have applied common English spellings (e.g. Tehran), and for transliterations, Persian pronunciations, thus 'Tehran' rather than 'Tihran', 'Taleban' rather than 'Taliban'.

Some readers will no doubt wonder about the use of the names 'Persia' and 'Iran' – whether they refer to one and the same place, and whether indeed 'Iran' is a new country founded on the ashes of the old. As should be apparent from the preceding text, the terms refer to the same country, but one, 'Persia', is the name accorded to the country by Western observers, inheriting the name from the Greek and Latin variants, while 'Iran' is the name by which the natives know the country.

The term 'Iran' has been in use since at least late antiquity and, even if the state disappeared, the cultural identity survived to re-emerge again in the sixteenth century with the establishment of the Safavid dynasty. By then, Western travellers were well aware of the name and recorded it. In 1934 (see chapter 2), the Iranian government instructed Western governments to desist from using 'Persia', but in the later twentieth century, this stricture was relaxed. Churchill insisted on the use of 'Persia' in all official documents because he felt, not without justification, that Iran would be too easily confused with Iraq – to the detriment, no doubt, of both! The *Daily Telegraph* persisted in using 'Persia' until 1979.

In choosing areas to focus on, I have tried to high-light those historical experiences that have shaped the current political landscape. In some cases, these are conscious influences frequently referred to by Iranians themselves – such as the Coup of 1953 – in other cases, there are events and developments which have perhaps more quietly yet durably informed opinion. Iranians can be a curiously ahistorical people, talking of events a hundred years ago as if they happened yesterday, although this does reflect the power of historical mythology (and selective memory) in shaping current attitudes.

This is why I have spent some time on the intellectual and political changes around the Constitutional Revolution in 1906, which were put into practice during the rule of Reza Shah. Indeed, the first fifty years of the twentieth century are in many ways the most productive period of political development, in which the foundations of the modern state were laid. An appreciation of the period is vital for any understanding of the current period.

Similarly, since the era of oil nationalization ranks so high in the popular memory, it is important for the reader to have an appreciation, as well as a more balanced understanding, of the achievements, perils and pitfalls of the last Shah, overthrown in 1979. Here the age-old dynamic between economic and political reform raises its head again, to be repeated, as will be seen, in the post-Islamic Revolutionary period.

Many histories of modern Iran tend to look at 1979, the onset of the Islamic Revolution, as year zero, with what preceded it as little more than a preamble. This is clearly nonsensical. The Islamic Revolution overthrew a monarchy, but it inherited a State built over half a century which was in large part founded on ideas shaped in the Constitutional Revolution. The social and economic developments realized in the post–1979 period were products of a revolution that started much earlier, and in many ways the history of the Islamic Republic is less one of how it sought to reimagine the reconciliation between tradition and modernity, and more one of how it has wasted its inheritance.

Indeed, the tragedy of modern Iran has been the inability of successive states to understand the integral relationship between political and economic reform, and that a modern economy requires transparency and accountability which reaches into political life and gives people a stake in the system that regulates their lives. If Enlightened Despotism was justified in the early parts of the century on account of the paucity of social and economic development, as society developed and people became more engaged and aware, this justification faded into irrelevance. The greatest criticism that can be directed at Mohammad Reza Shah is that he failed to live up to the promise of his father's generation and take Iran towards a democratic settlement. Impatient for progress, he ignored political imperatives and catastrophically failed to take the people with him, resulting in revolution, war and continued political turmoil.

The Islamic Republic too had its moment, but rather than take the path towards greater democratic accountability, however messy that appeared at times, it chose instead to reinstate autocracy, but this time on a scale few monarchs would have aspired to. This was a sacral monarchy with few inhibitions, constitutional or otherwise, who justified its policies on theocratic rather than national grounds. Far from being an authentic expression of Iranian national culture, the radical Islamist ideology of the Islamic Republic was taking the country in a wholly new direction, rooted in neither its recent history nor its culture.

1

A Constitutional Revolution
(1905–1913)

On 9 July 1906, Evelyn Grant Duff, the Secretary at the British Legation in Tehran received a letter from a senior Iranian cleric, seeking British assistance in the ongoing protests against the Shah. Grant Duff declined the invitation on the clear diplomatic basis that it would be inappropriate for the British government to engage in any activity against the Shah. In the following days, the protests that had been waxing and waning for the better part of seven months took a violent turn with the death of one of the protesters. The clerics decided that now was the time to leave the capital in order to prevent further bloodshed, but took the opportunity to convey 'the hope' to Grant Duff 'that they would have his sympathy in their struggle against cruelty and oppression'.[1] They were not to be disappointed. A week later, some 50 clerics and merchants took up residence in the British compound, building gradually over the next month to reach an astonishing total of 14,000 people. This figure was all the more remarkable when one considers that the population of Tehran at the time was probably not more than 250,000, and as such the gathering at the compound represented pretty much every politically active male in the city. It proved a turning point in the movement known to posterity as the Constitutional Revolution. Empowered by the *bast*, and after having nominated Grant Duff as their spokesman, the protesters succeeded in extracting from the Shah a constitution, an elected parliament (Majles), the separation of powers, and a recognition that the State would henceforth be governed by laws. It was the Revolution that established the template for modern Iran, changing the political landscape forever. Yet, seven months earlier, no one had foreseen it.

The Constitutional Revolution of 1906 was to transform the political landscape of modern Iran and to leave a profound imprint on the political psychology of the country to this day. Hailed by many Iranians as the first revolution of its type in the Middle East (it was in fact preceded by the failed Ottoman experiment in 1876), the Revolution provided Iran with its first constitution, limiting the power of the monarch with a separation of powers, and the establishment of the principle, if not the practice, of the rule of law. For all its practical limitations, it has set the template and become the reference point for all subsequent political activity and, as with many such political transformations, the catalyst for change appeared, to all intents and purposes, trivial.

Revolution

Customs collection was at this time the responsibility of a seemingly brusque Belgian official by the name of Naus. His harsh exactions, a vain attempt to stave off the insolvency of the State, were compounded by similar attempts by Iranian officials. What observers failed to appreciate was not only the depth of anger among the wider political populace, but the cogency of their ideas shaped over decades of frustration. The catalyst proved the most trivial of events: the beating of an aged 'Seyyed', a descendant of the family of the Prophet – not a particular rarity in the Muslim world, but of significance nonetheless because of the individual's age and pious associations.

This resulted in a protest among the leading clerics who decided to take *bast*, or sanctuary, in the Shah Abdol Azim shrine south of Tehran. The government sought to end the protest by offering the characteristic bribes and political sweeteners, but such was the anger of the clerics that they issued a sternly worded letter demanding redress of myriad political grievances and branded any cleric that gave in to the government's bribes 'as a traitor'.[2] The Shah made some vague promises about providing popular representation and addressing the deficiencies in the administration, especially justice, and contented himself that this appeared to have lanced the boil of revolt.

By mid-January 1906, the wind appeared to have been taken out of the protesters' sails and calm restored such that, when Arthur Hardinge sent his review of 1905, he made a passing comment about the political developments but concluded dryly that, if the country had not quite given up the ghost, it remained – in political terms at least – comatose.[3] The failure of British officials, with their multiple sources of intelligence in this period, to see the storm that was brewing remains a salutary lesson in the unpredictability of revolutions.

But, for all the apparent calm, there was a definite change of mood. 'In the capital itself the streets and the bazaars were quiet, but every day sermons were preached in the mosques, in which, as one of the popular party said, "what we hardly dared think a year ago was openly spoken".'[4] This moment, when the opposition to a government dare to think the unthinkable, and give voice to that which is generally left unspoken, is the watershed moment in any revolutionary endeavour. What was thought impossible becomes possible, and if the Babi Revolt had shattered the orthodoxies of the Shia faith, then the political reverberations of decades of failure and corruption were finally coming home to roost.

But there was yet another dimension to the changing political landscape: an international environment that was strangely sympathetic: 'To these strong motives must be added the wave of independence which was passing over the eastern part of Europe, and the added sense of dignity given to the Asiatic races by the victories of Japan. The great idol of autocracy which had overshadowed the world was being shattered from without and undermined from within.'[5] This great idol of autocracy was, of course, Russia, who not only had suffered an unprecedented defeat at the hands of

Japan in the Russo-Japanese War (1904–5), but was subsequently embroiled in a revolution of its own – in 1905 – which the Tsar was in the process of violently suppressing, leading a number of revolutionaries, especially those from the Caucasus, to head south.[6]

The next stage was for visible fractures in the governing elite to make themselves felt. There were many members of the clerical and intellectual elite (including a fair number of landed nobility) who had already broken ranks but, while the governing – aristocratic – elite remained united and loyal, the crown felt little inclination to move on its vague allusions to reform. But as winter gave way to spring and the government found itself confronting increasingly aggressive sermons, the decision was taken to convene a 'Council' through which matters could be discussed with a degree of visible gravity.

This was in many ways simply an attempt to show unity at the top, but it backfired when one official broke ranks and decried the corruption that had infected the country. But a far more serious fracture was about to afflict the governing elite, in the person of the Shah himself who, in May, suffered from a paralytic stroke, turning a lethargic existence into a stupor that could barely respond to the urgent matters of the day. To better protect the health of His Majesty, the highly reactionary Minister of Court took care to edit out the worst news that might reach him. The Shah was dispatched for convalescence to the country, and calm was once again restored.

But, in a pattern all too familiar, the calm was to be disrupted by yet another government attempt to restore order on its own terms. Irritated by the continued critical preaching of the senior clerics, a further attempt was made to arrest one of them – in this case, once again, an elderly Seyyed. Alerted to the attempted arrest by a passing woman, the mob moved to release the Seyyed and, in the ensuing brawl, the commander of the troops ordered his men to fire on the crowd. They refused. The officer then proceeded to shoot the Seyyed dead.

This breakdown in authority and solitary act of violence signalled a significant escalation of the protest. Attempts to quell the momentum had failed and the anger of the crowd now made itself felt, with an attack on the guardhouse resulting in further casualties and the rout of the soldiers. The initiative had passed to the protesters, who proved to be much better organized than the authorities had imagined. Discontent spread to the bazaar, and the senior clergy took refuge in the Great Mosque, which was promptly put under siege by the authorities.

After some negotiation, the senior clerics were allowed to leave for the religious city of Qom, provided 'they were not accompanied by the people', leaving Tehran bereft of 'religious guidance' or the 'possibility of carrying out any legal transactions'.[7] If calm was not fully restored, the initiative appeared to be back in the hands of the government who, contrary to general expectation, were no more inclined to respect religious sanctities than anyone else. It is at this critical stage that the protesters resorted to seeking *bast* in the British Legation compound at Golhak.

As political gatherings go, there will have been few to match it as the great and good of the city met to discuss strategy and define their aims. They were clear that the British diplomat Grant Duff would be their official interlocutor with the authorities. The direct involvement of a British diplomat in the ensuing negotiations has naturally been the source of subsequent controversy, but it was a testament to the very real influence of British political ideas on the constitutional movement, and to the fact that there was a complete collapse in faith in the Iranian authorities to deliver on their promises. Such was the gulf of mistrust that the protesters at one stage insisted that any agreement had to be guaranteed by the British monarch, a proposition that Grant Duff unsurprisingly rejected.

Subsequent critics of the Constitutional Revolution, notably in the Islamic Republic, have argued that this is when the constitutional movement was diverted from its true path of religious government, as British officials surreptitiously changed the demands of the protesters from that of *mashru'eh* (the implementation of Sharia law) to *mashruteh*, a 'constitution', through the insertion of a wayward 't'.[8] Quite apart from highlighting the paranoid mind of the critic, this says little for their estimation of those Iranians who had occupied the Legation, many of whom were clerics.

Far from being a gullible rabble, the protesters impressed their hosts with their discipline:

> Their conduct was most orderly. The crowd of refugees were organized by the heads of the guilds, who took measures to prevent any unauthorized persons from entering the Legation grounds. Tents were put up and regular feeding places and times of feeding were provided for. The expense was borne by the principal merchants. No damage of a wilful character was done to the garden, although, of course, every semblance of a bed was trampled out of existence, and the trees still bear pious inscriptions cut in the bark. Colonel Douglas, the Military Attaché, kept watch over the Legation buildings, but no watch was needed. Discipline and order were maintained by the refugees themselves.[9]

After extended negotiations and no little prevarication by the court, the Shah consented to the establishment of a National Assembly and Courts of Justice. The *mujtahids* agreed to return from Qom and the protesters left the Legation. On 19 August, a month after the *bast* had been initiated, a meeting was held with the Shah, as part of wider ceremonies celebrating the establishment of the new order, during which the ailing monarch expressed the hope that his subjects would continue to serve him. The response of a number of the senior clergy, much to the astonishment of many of the observers, was that 'they did not serve him but themselves and the nation'.[10]

By the end of the year, Muzaffar al-Din Shah was persuaded to sign the new and somewhat embryonic constitution into law before finally expiring on 8 January 1907. As the new British Minister trumpeted in his review of the year, 'The year 1906 has been a very important epoch in Persian history, for it has brought with it the introduction of parliamentary institutions.'[11]

A Long Shadow

It had been a remarkable turn of events. The Constitutional Revolution of 1906 was a watershed moment in modern Iranian history, and it cast a long shadow on subsequent politics. Not only was it transformative, but it served as a reference point for most subsequent movements. Above all, it carried within it many of the hallmarks of the success (and failure) of Iranian protest movements that would come to litter the political landscape over the next century. The power of ideas, the unity of purpose – drawing support from key sectors in society: intellectuals, the merchants (*bazaaris*) and the clergy (*ulema*) – and an organization and discipline which was often belied by the size of the crowd.

This was no rabble, despite the characterization by the authorities who sought to sow dissension and doubt – to divide so that they might better rule. But, faced with a unity of purpose, it was the authorities who appeared to lack coherence, were wracked by doubt and dissension, and if the lynchpin of the system, the monarch, was himself incapacitated, this incoherence would be reinforced.

The advance of technology – in this case, the tele-graph network and printing (though this was largely conducted from abroad at this stage) – helped to cement social cohesion and communication; and then, last but by no means least, was the international environment and the dynamics which might help or hinder a movement. In this particular case, there was an unusual conjunction of events: the preoccupation of the Russians with their own problems, and the fact that, in the absence of the British Minister, decisions on the ground were being taken by a relatively junior diplomat.

Indeed, as the newly appointed British Minister, Cecil Spring Rice, was to write to Sir Edward Grey – the new Liberal foreign secretary who came into office in 1906 – rarely had British prestige in Iran been higher. The new constitution was modelled on that of Belgium, itself a redaction of the uncodified British constitution. Iranian political thinkers had contem-plated and studied both the French and the British political systems and had decided that the system of constitutional monarchy with a parliament served their interests best. The composition of Britain, as a multi-ethnic 'national state', also served a better model to draw on as Iran's nationalist ideologues sought to transition Iran from an imperial state to a national one. In a very real sense, Britain had been midwife to the birth of modern Iran.

The tragedy for the constitutionalists was that many of the circumstances that had helped to propel them to success were about to change, and perhaps the most immediately serious was the position of Britain. It was much to the constitutionalists' advantage that communications between Tehran and London still took several weeks, especially if one was seeking to send a detailed dispatch rather than a telegram. Grant Duff was therefore left to make key decisions without recourse to London, and it is unlikely that Edward Grey would have sanctioned the *bast* had he been apprised of the prospect beforehand.

British involvement in the constitutional movement horrified him, in part because he remained convinced that the Revolution would achieve little more than to create further instability. But, more to the point, this instability would only encourage Russian aggrandizement. Grey's priority was to seek a rapprochement with Russia in the interests of British security in Europe, and the Constitutional Revolution proved an 'inconvenient truth' he would rather wish away. Dismissing the possibility of its success, he moved swiftly to reach a detente with Russia, which would settle outstanding disputes in Asia, protect India and, above all, protect Britain, which he now tied into a Continental commitment with France and the Russian Empire.

The 1907 Anglo-Russian Convention not only settled disputes across Asia, it also split Iran into respective spheres of influence, assuring either party of no interference in the other zone. The difficulty for Grey was that the spheres of influence agreed effectively put all the populated parts of northern Iran into the Russian sphere while reserving eastern Baluchestan for Britain – ostensibly for the defence of India – though even the British Indian government found the agreement both tawdry and self-defeating.

Perhaps the most striking aspect of the agreement was that the British sphere did not even include those parts of south-western Iran where British geologists were prospecting for oil – a reminder perhaps of how irrelevant Persian oil was at this stage. For the constitutionalists, who soon became aware of the convention, the agreement was the worst possible outcome insofar as it appeared to give a resurgent and highly reactionary Russian Empire carte blanche to interfere in the politics of Iran without fear of British obstruction. Spring Rice pointedly remarked to Grey that, in agreeing to the convention, 'we are regarded as having betrayed the Persian people'.[12] It would not be the last time that Iranian rights would be sacrificed on the altar of wider security imperatives.

But if Grey had been too eager in his dismissal of the prospects for success – and perhaps hastened their failure through his rapprochement with Russia – he was not wrong in his belief that the constitutionalists faced a daunting challenge in turning their ideals into a practical reality. The deputies who were elected to the first parliament attended with considerable enthusiasm but little experience of what was expected. Foroughi produced a handbook for them explaining the basics of the legislative process and the differences between the French and British constitutional systems.

But enthusiasm proved a poor substitute for capacity and the deputies soon discovered that ideas were empty without the means to implement them. Iran had no government in the modern sense of the term. Its bureaucracy was small, feeble and wracked by corruption, while the government lacked the means to enforce its will. There was no administration to speak of and, while deputies outlined increasingly grandiose plans for the development of the country, it soon became apparent that there was no realistic idea of how to finance these projects. The initial idea had been to lay the plans before the monarch who would then, in a curious reversal of the process that developed in Europe, proceed to fund the projects.

But the new monarch, Mohammad Ali Shah, had no intention of being so accommodating, and it was clear that a system of taxation would be required to finance the innovative and, in many ways, highly progressive projects. Quite apart from establishing a sound administration, the deputies wanted to improve transport infrastructure (railways were key) and fund nationwide education, as well as develop a distinct judiciary. But the difficulties of establishing a modern state from scratch soon became apparent. Take education or the judiciary: there were neither teachers nor a basic infrastructure (beyond seminaries and the occasional foreign or missionary school); there were no law codes or lawyers. As Foroughi was to reflect many years later, the task ahead of the deputies was considerably more daunting than many of them had imagined.[13] All the more so because there were many within the establishment who were against any type of change or innovation, still less a change that appeared to have been adopted wholesale from Christian Europe.

The 'Reactionary' party, as their opponents derided them, gathered round the new monarch, who had no intention of honouring his father's (lackadaisical) commitment to the new constitutional order – and, moreover, he could now count on the support of a reinvigorated Russia, with Tsar Nicholas in no mood to tolerate a revolutionary movement that would enhance British prestige. These forces were aided by the fact that the revolutionaries themselves were divided.

Having succeeded, Iran's revolutionaries were not at all clear what to do with their success. The plans they had were clearly unrealistic, but it was also apparent that the broad coalition that had triumphed against the monarchy had differing views about how to proceed. Two key fractures began to emerge. The first lay with the awkward preponderance of deputies from Tehran over the rest of the country. This anomaly was exacerbated by the fact that the deputies for the first parliament decided to initiate proceedings – on the basis that a quorum had been achieved – before any deputies from the provinces had arrived.

Since many of the deputies from Tehran were more radical than those from the provinces, this ensured that the programme put forward jarred with many incoming deputies, not least because it had been initiated without them. But, more pertinently, these more radical deputies had decided to lay out plans without fully implementing aspects of the constitution that required all prospective laws to be vetted by a council of senior clerical jurists. The failure to apply this important concession to the religious leadership of the country, many of whom had been key supporters of the constitution, was regarded as a slight and a serious political miscalculation.

Traditionalists started to gather around the Shah and attempts were made to suffocate the Revolution, resulting in a protracted period of instability. That the British, through the Anglo-Russian convention, basically gave the Russians a free hand to derail the constitution and create the very instability that Grey had predicted, was a political sleight of hand that few revolutionaries missed. One notable revolutionary, Hasan Taqizadeh, who was a correspondent of Edward Browne, travelled to Britain in 1908 to make an impassioned plea for support. His 'Appeal to England' was a masterful exposition of the situation, outlined Russia's strategy in Iran and reiterated that 'The Persian Constitution . . . was in an especial sense the spiritual child of Great Britain',[14] adding for good measure that the constitutionalists were not seeking British intervention, only assistance in preventing the Russians from intervening: 'We neither ask nor hope for help from foreign powers, but only entreat them to refrain from intervening against us in support of the ancient tyranny.'[15]

Ultimately, Mohammad Ali Shah's attempt to close down the parliament was reversed as rival forces converged on the capital and forced the Shah's abdication in favour of his son Ahmad Shah in 1909. The Revolution had been saved from extinction. Reactionaries were pursued and executed – notably, the cleric Fazlollah Nuri (later to be lionized by hardline supporters of the Islamic Revolution in 1979) – and the constitution clarified to remove anomalies, most obviously the dominance of Tehran.

More dramatically, recognized religious minorities – Zoroastrians, Christians and Jews (though not Bahais) – were granted representation, and the limited franchise was expanded by reducing the value of property required for eligibility to vote. At the same time, many of the fundamental problems of how to translate ideas into action remained. The new Iranian government recognized that sound financial administration was an essential prerequisite to meaningful progress, and began to scout around for help in this regard, turning to the United States.

The Americans, anxious not to offend either the British or the Russians, decided that discretion was the better part of valour and declined any formal association, but allowed a banker by the name of Morgan Shuster to be sent to Iran in a private capacity, where he would take up his new post in the employ of the Iranian government. Shuster's depiction of Iran in this period – he arrived in May 1911 – is worth recounting in full:

> Imagine if you will, a fast decaying government amid whose tottering ruins a heterogeneous collection of Belgian customs officers, Italian Gendarmes, German artillery sergeants, French savants, doctors, professors, and councillors of state, Austrian military instructors, English bank clerks, Turkish and Armenian courtiers, and last, but not least, a goodly sprinkling of Russian Cossack officers, tutors, and drill instructors all go through their daily task of giving the Imperial Persian Government a strong shove toward bankruptcy, with a sly side push in the direction of their own particular political or personal interests. In this pleasant diversion, the gentlemen and even the ladies of the foreign legations were somewhat peacefully engaged, when several unfortunate Americans landed on Persian soil with the truly extraordinary idea that they were to be employed under the orders of the Persian Government.[16]

The Europeans treated Shuster's mission with a good deal of mirth, and even Shuster was moved to comment that Iranian politics resembled nothing less than an 'opera bouffe', with individuals changing their politics as expedience dictated.[17] It was difficult enough, complained Shuster, to understand the political landscape of Iran, let alone the chaos of the Iranian finances, mired as it all was in deep factionalism reinforced by the choice interventions of foreign powers.

It was clear to Shuster that neither the British, nor particularly the Russians, were anxious for him to succeed lest their own influence wither, and with bitter regret Shuster found his contract abruptly terminated within a year. By 1912, with the closure of the second parliament (each parliament served for two years at this stage), the reality, if not the dream, of the Constitutional Revolution came to a stuttering halt. By this stage, the Russians were engaged in a large-scale military intervention bombarding the shrine of Imam Reza in Mashhad, killing some fifty unarmed pilgrims and taking harsh retribution on 'revolutionaries' in Tabriz, as described by Shuster in graphic detail.

On the eve of the Great War, in August 1914, central government had all but collapsed, and whole tales of anarchy have often been exaggerated, but there was certainly a very real threat to the territorial existence of Iran as centrifugal forces took hold. The Great War was to see Iranian neutrality ignored – partly by the Iranians themselves as different factions sought to align with rival belligerents – and the country fought over with devastating consequences for the social and economic fabric of the country.

Oil

Behind the political din of the Constitutional Revolution, there were other developments taking place that would transform the economic landscape of the country with consequences as far-reaching as those of the events of 1906. This was the discovery of oil. Oil transformed Iran's economic potential, turned her from an imperial 'buffer' state to a strategic asset of considerable importance in her own right and, in the guise of the Anglo-Persian (later Anglo-Iranian) Oil Company, provided Iran with her first industrial experience. Although few paid any attention to the prospects for oil in Iran in the first decade of the twentieth century, the emergence of an oil industry was to shape profoundly the development of the modern Iranian State and cast a long, and not entirely benign, shadow on the political landscape.

Given the subsequent importance of oil, it is perhaps counter-intuitive to appreciate that prospects for its exploitation were not considered propitious, despite the fact that there were obvious deposits. The difficulty lay in finding deposits that were accessible and economically viable. This was in no small part due to the fact that the environment was especially severe, with few, if any, transportation links: a salutary reminder of the economic underdevelopment of the Iranian state. Unlike in Egypt and the Ottoman Empire, there was negligible development of railways, roads were scarce and poorly maintained, and the economic landscape was fractured.

The 'Guarded Domains' of Iran represented an imperial agglomeration of distinct political and economic territories, and while they were bound by a shared culture, reinforced by modern communications (the telegraph), economic integration remained some way off. This was far from being a 'single market'. Prospecting for oil in the southern and western parts of the country was therefore considered both unattractive and hazardous work, all the more so as political authority began to wane.

Nonetheless, in 1901, the British-Australian entrepreneur William Knox-D'Arcy signed a concession with the Iranian government for the exploration and exploitation of oil in southern Iran. Like previous concessions, this one was to last 60 years and the down-payment amounted to £40,000, a not insignificant sum on the face of it – but generous terms in light of what was to develop. Muzaffar al-Din Shah does not seem to have regarded the prospects as good, which probably explained the characteristically indolent approach to the negotiations, treating the establishment of an oil industry as little different to previous concessions.

The most egregious part of the concession as far as the Iranians were concerned was the agreement that any successful enterprise would pay royalties to the Iranian government commensurate with 16 per cent of the profits, a concept which even the official historian of BP considered 'vague', and which was, unsurprisingly, to rankle with the Iranians going forward.[18] That said, Muzaffar al-Din Shah's scepticism was not initially misplaced, as Knox D'Arcy's team struggled to strike oil, only achieving success some 7 years later in 1908, after considerable further outlay. Indeed, Knox D'Arcy was on the verge of giving up when oil was struck and, by this stage, he had sold most of his rights to Burmah Oil.[19]

Despite all this, the British government initially took remarkably little interest in this new development. By the eve of the Great War, as the Company began to establish itself, it was Churchill's decision, as First Lord of the Admiralty, to seek a golden share in the company in return for considerable government investment. In agreeing to this, the Company, and by extension Iran, became a vital strategic asset for Britain. Churchill was anxious to provide reliable supplies of oil to the navy, which was steadily converting from coal to oil, and he was able to sign an agreement with the company providing for a doubling of the company's capital in return for the appointment of two *ex officio* directors who ostensibly held a veto over the company's decisions.

Churchill's new arrangement was to prove something of a double-edged sword. The company was henceforth viewed by its critics as an arm of the British government, and indeed any errors in judgement were promptly blamed on Whitehall. But such were the concerns about government interference in 'free enterprise' that the government 'veto' was strictly limited to strategic issues, essentially to ensure that the company was not sold off to foreign powers. These strict limitations, conveyed in a confidential letter, were the basis on which Parliament approved the agreement, and subsequent governments were to become increasingly frustrated by an arrangement in which they took the blame for actions they had very little formal capacity to influence.

The establishment of the Anglo-Persian Oil Company and the involvement of the British government were to prove turning points no less significant than the Constitutional Revolution. The latter transformed the political landscape, while the former revolutionized the economic one. Industry had arrived in Iran. In both cases, the architecture of the Qajar State was poorly prepared. Modernity had arrived with a bang. Change was coming.

2

The Rise and Rule of Reza Shah (1914–1940)

Iran faced the onset of the Great War in political disarray. That a coherent community existed at all was testament to the tremendous power and richness of its cultural inheritance. Despite this, there was nothing inevitable about the continued existence of the Iranian State, and a major anxiety among the statesmen of this period was the very real possibility that 'Iran' might be absorbed by greater powers or simply fragmented. These fears were to become existential by the end of the war when the fate of the Russian and Ottoman empires became apparent. That Iranian statesmen managed Iran's transition from an imperial to a legally recognized 'national' state is an achievement all too underappreciated to this day.

The Constitutional Revolution had been high on ideas and low on pragmatism. There was appreciation of how the many ideas that were drawn up for the development of the State might be implemented. And with the departure of Shuster, factional infighting began to dominate the landscape. Central government lost any pretence to nationwide authority. The immediate consequences of this were probably not as devastating as some writers have suggested, for the simple reason that Iran remained a patchwork of different authorities (and ecosystems) bound under the nominal authority of the monarchy. That said, the Great War would accentuate the inherent weaknesses exposed by the fragmentation of power, and few – even in the Iranian government – took Iran's proclaimed neutrality seriously.

The Ottomans and the Russians contested the Caucasus and, in efforts to outflank each other, moved progressively southwards to send troops into parts of north and north-western Iran. The paucity of communications meant that troop concentrations were light but the damage to local economies was immense, as troops looted the countryside. The worst initial offenders were the Ottomans, but they were swiftly followed by the Russians, especially with the onset of the Russian Revolution in 1917 and the complete breakdown of discipline among the Russian Cossack Brigade following the departure of their officers, providing openings for aspiring and ambitious Iranian junior officers to rise up the ranks.

It was left to the third foreign power, Britain, to step in and restore a measure of order to the Cossack Brigade, providing vital subsidies. By the end of the war, the British found themselves in occupation of a country of which parts had been desolated by war and famine and the onset of Spanish flu. Although there are no reliable statistics, contemporaries were of little doubt that the west of the country had suffered badly.

The Anglo-Persian Agreement

It is nonetheless testament to the resilience of the State that the government organized and dispatched a delegation to the Paris Peace Conference of 1919. Possessed of a remarkable self-confidence, the delegation sought vast financial reparations and territorial restitution of lands separated from Iran over the previous century. If the former had some merit, the latter claims were treated as ridiculous, including as they did much of central Asia and Caucasus.

Curzon was unsurprisingly dismissive of a Persian delegation who sought a seat at the victor's table and, regarding Iran as part of his own diplomatic patrimony, was not about to allow an international consortium to participate in its economic regeneration. Deemed by his compatriots to have an unhealthy obsession with Persia, her predicament was just the opportunity Curzon needed to put his 'altruistic' imperialism into effect, a test case to prove the naysayers wrong and, in his eyes, to compensate for the errors of 1907. The resultant Anglo-Persian Agreement was to prove, contrary to Curzon's wishes, one of the more controversial episodes in Anglo-Iranian history.

Reflecting many of the demands made by the Iranian government for economic assistance, this would be a bilateral agreement which envisaged a loan of £2 million, along with British assistance with the army, finances and transport infrastructure. In light of the wider territorial changes taking place, it made an important if undervalued commitment to Iran's territorial sovereignty, much mocked by nationalists but significant in the context of the times.

The problem lay less in what it stipulated, which some felt came precariously close to turning Iran into a British protectorate, than in the bribes demanded – and reluctantly acceded to by Curzon – to achieve it. But in the immediate term, there were more serious objections from both abroad and within the British government, which was anxious to reduce costs and avoid unnecessary commitments. Observers began to cast around for an altogether different type of solution.

The Man on Horseback

For the British military, anxious to disengage from Iran, and lacking any enthusiasm for Curzon's plans, the installation of a sympathetic 'strong man' appeared to be the ideal solution. Having assumed control of the Cossack Brigade and become acquainted with their Persian officers, one man stood out: Reza Khan. Reza Khan, driven by an ingrained – if at times raw – sense of nationalism, had already shown himself ambitious for power long before the British appeared on the scene, and British interest was drawn to him because he seemed to be a man of action. He was less a British creation and more a man whose time had come.

This was also reflected in the views of Iranian intellectuals, who, made despondent by the turn of events after the Constitutional Revolution, were casting around for a saviour. The priority was the establishment of good governance and, reflecting on the European experience, they settled on the realization that what Iran needed was an Enlightened Despot: a ruler who could force the pace of change and create a modern state that would in time become democratized.

Thus, in February 1921, with the politics of the country inert and the Anglo-Persian Agreement still-born, a group of conspirators led by the pro-British journalist and intellectual Seyyed Zia Tabatabai, with the Cossack Brigade under the command of Reza Khan in full support, marched on Tehran to overthrow the corrupt administration and establish a national unity government. British officials on the ground, anxious to remove the burden of Iran from their shoulders, were much relieved, if not a little satisfied, and no doubt shed few tears when the new government rejected the Agreement once and for all, a development which only added to Curzon's anguish.

Within six months of the coup, Reza Khan had dispensed with Seyyed Zia and had manoeuvred himself gradually and with a methodical calculation from head of the armed forces to Minister of War and, finally, to Prime Minister. His first task was to restore central government authority, and to this end he forged a military force, with parliament's agreement, that could bring various centrifugal forces to heel.

The most important development in this regard was the restoration of authority in the south-western province of Khuzestan, where the British had cultivated the support of the local Arab sheikh, Khazal of Mohammarah, to provide security for the Anglo-Persian Oil Company and its burgeoning oil refinery at Abadan. Reza Khan was determined to bring the wayward sheikh under government control and to prevent any possibility of the British treating the area as autonomous or, heaven forbid, independent under their protection. In perhaps one of the more important decisions relating to Iran in this period, the British Minister, Sir Percy Loraine, reported to London that it should put its weight behind Reza Khan, as the best prospect for a stable and sustainable Iran. Loraine's advice empowered the Iranian State, empowered Reza Khan and ensured that oil revenue continued to flow into the coffers of the Iranian treasury – vital if the modernization plans were to be realized.

Having established internal order, Reza Khan was now in a strong position to begin the process of state construction that had evaded the constitutionalists for nearly two decades. Supported by a small, if favoured and loyal, army, Iran's 'Peter the Great' embarked on his great project supported and encouraged by intel-lectuals who could finally see their aspirations being realized. For Iran's impatient nationalists seized by the 'fierce urgency of now', if Reza Khan's methods occasionally left a lot to be desired, they were a price worth paying for the changes to come. The ends would justify the means. And the ends were nothing less than a complete transformation of the State and a revolution of the mind.

In the fourth and fifth parliamentary sessions (from 1921 to 1925), the new Prime Minister introduced conscription, and took steps to rationalize the civil service with competitive examinations, but it was the fifth parliament in 1924 which might be said to have inaugurated the modern state, with a series of important reforms including: the adoption of surnames and the need to obtain a birth certificate; standardized weights and measures; two-year conscription; and the adoption of the Persian solar calendar (as opposed to the Muslim lunar calendar) as the official calendar of the state, dated from the migration of the Prophet but with the addition of distinct Persian month names from the pre-Islamic era. The lunar calendar continued to be in use for all religious festivals and, of course, Iranians were also familiar with the Gregorian (Christian) calendar.

This new calendar remains in use in Iran to this day. The attempt by Reza Khan's son, Mohammad Reza Shah, to recalibrate the calendar to start with the accession of Cyrus the Great in 559 BC (as opposed to the Hijra of the Prophet) proved a misguided experiment which lasted no more than two years. The Islamic revolutionaries in 1979 made no attempt to change this calendar – a reminder perhaps that the Revolution of 1979 may have overthrown the Shah, but it left much of the architecture of the state built by Reza Shah intact.

Reza Khan, as he eyed the throne, decided to choose a suitably archaic surname for himself – Pahlavi. The term was traditionally used to denote the Middle Persian language spoken during the Parthian and Sasanian eras (c.250 BC – AD 640) but some also suggested that the 'Pahlavis' were one of the seven great families of pre-Islamic Iran. It was a bold association to make with an invented genealogy which was second to none, and it indicated that the model for the 'strong State' that he sought to emulate was that of the Sasanian Empire.

But before he could make his bid for the throne, Reza Khan had to reconcile several vested interests that might be opposed to the deposition of the Qajars. The first were the clergy, though how he addressed this conundrum was to suggest that he was considering abolishing the monarchy altogether and establishing a republic on the lines of Mustafa Kemal's in Turkey. While some thought that, as in Turkey, this would be a fast track to dictatorship, others expressed the far greater horror that, like Turkey, this would mean the end of religion. Suitably frightened, the clergy, unlike their progeny some fifty years later, stressed that, given the options before them, Reza Khan taking on the mantle and prerogatives of monarchy was by far the best route, since a monarch, subject to Islamic strictures, could not be despotic and, moreover, was obligated in the coronation oath to support the faith.

The second group was a number of deputies, some of whom were part of the extended Qajar aristocracy. Among these was the young veteran of the

Constitutional Revolution, Dr Mohammad Mosaddeq, who protested that, since the constitution stated that a monarch must reign but not rule, and was absolved of any responsibility, it would be a tragedy for the state if the active and energetic Prime Minister became Shah, and thereby deprived the state of his talents. Unsurprisingly, this ingenious argument did not get far. Others, including Taqizadeh – who argued that a special constitutional commission had to be set up, insisting that parliament had no right to dismiss a monarch – found themselves outvoted by a parliament now largely filled with Reza Khan loyalists. As such, with the requisite last-minute arm twisting, the parliament finally persuaded itself to depose the Qajars and establish a new 'national' monarchy in the person and family of Reza Pahlavi, who in 1925 became Reza Shah.

Reza Shah

Reza Shah's rule (1925–41) has tended to polarize opinion. His supporters see him as the founder of modern Iran, the builder of the modern Iranian state and all that flowed from that. His detractors, on the other hand, saw him as a despot and a bully. His determined intention to secularize the country and marginalize the clergy have earned their permanent enmity and, during the Islamic Revolution, his tomb was swiftly targeted for destruction. Yet it is fair to say that time has been kind to Reza Shah and his legacy, not least because he achieved a great deal in a relatively short space of time and much of what he built has lasted,[1] while his contempt for the clergy, criticized in the past, is regarded by most Iranians, after four decades of clerical government, as one of the highlights of his rule.

But even this sympathetic view must acknowledge that Reza Shah was supported by some very capable people. In this sense, Reza Shah was a continuation and part fulfilment of the Constitutional Revolution. Certainly, for all his tendency to aggrandize credit for any and all achievement to his own person, he always identified himself with the Constitution, even if his understanding of the law was frequently found wanting. But an understanding of the achievements of this short period in modern Iranian history requires an appreciation of its constitutional context and of the many revolutionaries who comprised the team of bureaucrats that became the velvet glove around Reza Shah's iron fist.

Three individuals stand out who, in the early years, formed a highly effective triumvirate: Abdol-Hossein Teymourtash, the debonair and flamboyant Minister of Court – an aristocrat from Khorasan in the east, known for both working hard and playing hard; Prince Firuz Nosret al-Dowleh, another aristocrat and scion of the Qajar house who became Minister of Finance; and, last but by no means least, Ali Akbar Davar. All three were to come to an unfortunate end: Firuz and Teymourtash in part because the increasingly paranoid dynast worried about their political ambitions, Davar from sheer exhaustion.

To Davar fell the responsibility for one of the two great changes that were to occur in this period – the establishment of a modern legal system and judiciary. Setting up a modern legal system had been a key goal and aspiration of the constitutionalists. But how did one construct a legal edifice, system and institutions from scratch? Iran had no legal codes, lawyers or indeed judges, so one would need to send people abroad to train them. This would, by its very nature, be a slow process – and then there was the opposition of the clergy, who argued for the primacy of Islamic law and viewed with some reservation the importation of civil codes and family law.

For all the desire for change, the catalyst came from a distinctly nationalist and practical imperative. Reza Shah was anxious to remove the various capitulatory rights which had been accorded to foreign powers over the previous century and which had enabled them to trade in Iran with particular advantages, not least the right to be tried in separate courts under European law. Few were willing to operate in Iran and be subject to what was widely considered to be an arbitrary legal system.

Reza Shah was informed that the abolition of capitulatory rights could only occur when a comparable legal system had been established in Iran. He was resolved to task Davar with establishing a functioning judiciary and legal system within a year. Davar was, of course, building on work already drafted, but the practical implementation was extraordinarily ambitious and the fact that something was established by 1928 was no mean achievement. It would be erroneous to suggest that the work was complete, but the essential foundations had been laid. That said, it soon became apparent that the judicial system was far from independent – but, above all, while the rights of the State had been fairly well established, the rights of the individual had yet to be fully addressed, ensuring that the legal apparatus in this period remained very much at the service of the State.

For all these important shortfalls, however, there were some striking developments in penal policy, especially when considered in the context of the Qajar inheritance. Under the Qajar State, corporal punishment and violence against prisoners and convicts was very much part of the routine of the judicial process. Now, while those who attempted to harm the king – spies – might expect the full weight of the State to fall upon them (and petty criminals might still expect to be roughly treated), others who held different, even seditious, points of view were treated in a wholly novel way more in tune with the Enlightenment.

Indeed, political prisoners who had been incarcerated because of their communist sympathies found prison a much transformed place, even civilized in its attitude, with considerable time for reading and discussion. Reza Shah, who found such approaches incomprehensible, was informed by guards and wardens that, while such individuals might be misguided, they remained at heart Iranians who should be persuaded of the errors of their ways rather than physically maltreated. In the words of one of the prisoners, Iran's new judicial and police officials were 'European trained products of the Constitutional Revolution'.[2]

This Enlightenment imperative also shaped the second major pillar of State reform in this period: education. The constitutionalists had been very keen on the establishment of nationwide free education in order to develop the new citizenry that would come to populate the new Iran. These modern Iranians would be forged on a new anvil of nationalism, instilled with pride in the past and confidence in the future. To be sure, Reza Shah's preference, being as it was a product of the parade ground rather than the seminar room, was for the creation of patriotic and obedient subjects, while the constitutionalists sought citizens who could engage in and contribute to the political process. There was, nonetheless, sufficient initial overlap in the distinctive ambitions for the contradictions not to impede progress.

As with the judiciary, it was difficult to know where to start, not least because the problems were of a magnitude greater: seeking to educate a population in which literacy was negligible. The first issue was that of training sufficient teachers and, in the first instance, as with much else, the decision was taken to send promising candidates abroad. These initial cohorts would form the nucleus of the teaching cadres who would in the first instance train further teachers at home. It soon became apparent that practicalities dictated a focus on primary and tertiary education, with perhaps the greatest strides made in the latter.

In 1934, with a determination which even his detractors found impressive, Reza Shah founded Tehran University by amalgamating the earlier colleges – such as that of Political Science and Law – with new faculties. Reza Shah was, needless to say, driven not only by pride but by a misplaced conviction that educating Iranians at home would shield them from wayward political ideas abroad. This was to prove, in very short order, a bad case of wishful thinking.

But there were also far more fundamental changes in train, in the form of language reform. Historians, often taking their lead from the Turkish example where the entire alphabet was replaced, have tended to misunderstand the process at work in Iran and to assume the changes were ideologically driven by an enthusiasm for purging the language of its Arabic loanwords. There were undoubtedly individuals whose enthusiasm for Persianization took them to ridiculous ends in their zeal to invent new words. But the truth is that most serious scholars with an eye on policy could see the impracticality and sheer absurdity of ridding Persian of up to 40 per cent of its vocabulary, much of which had been part of the linguistic landscape for so long that it could not real-istically be considered 'Arabic'.

Indeed, a far bigger issue for many people was not Arabic but French, as those Iranians returning from abroad sought to stress their cosmopolitanism by referencing French words wherever possible. The literary satirist Jamalzadeh joked, in an article, that it was well known that Esperanto 'is already spoken in Iran',[3] and it is worth noting that Reza Shah himself would become particularly incensed at the use of for-eign words and, on occasion, invented archaisms that he regarded – rightly – as pretentious.

Reza Shah was regularly criticized by his detrac-tors as an illiterate Cossack, as some of his initial backers lamented the brusque manner and occasion-ally brutish style of his approach. But while he did emanate from the Cossack Brigade, and was not a man of letters, he was far from illiterate. His military background gave him a deep distrust of the flowery diction of bureaucrats, and he was clearly allergic to obfuscation. But this also meant that he shared and could understand the desire of many reformers to simplify the language.

If the ambition was to educate the population, one had to simplify and regularize the language. New grammars would be required, along with dictionar-ies of accepted spellings. The poetic licence of the past in which rules were adjusted to accommodate the rhyme had to be replaced with something more straightforward and more rigorous. All this, of course, was eminently understandable to someone like Reza Shah, but was also of immense practicality to the educational planners of the period.

Complex constructions were to be replaced by simplified neologisms which drew together linguistic components that were both logical and comprehensible to the wider public. So, the Arabic compound for enlightened thinker – *munavvar al-fekr* – was rephrased as *roshan* (light) *fekr* (thinker). The French word for a university was discarded in favour of *danesh* (learning) *gah* (place), while an airport became *forud-gah* (the place of landing). Easy to learn constructions like these soon became accepted and commonplace, a testament to the skill of the wordsmiths. Not all revisions landed successfully and those failures were quickly discarded. Some French words, of course, remained – such as *merci*, for 'thank you' – and many terms for new technology were simply appropriated, such as 'telephone'.

But perhaps the clearest indication that this was a pragmatic and not an ideological project was the fact that a number of Arabic words that could have been very simple to change were left as they were – not least the term for the language itself: *farsi*. The fact that Iranians spoke Farsi and not Parsi (i.e. Persian) was due to the invading Muslim Arabs having no 'P' in their alphabet and thus using 'F' instead. The southern Iranian province of Pars, from where the ancient Persian dynasties had emanated, thus became Fars and the language Farsi. It would not have been a difficult task to change this (as some have done today), but the fact is, it was not touched. Similarly with the 'Persian Gulf', towards which the Iranians remain immensely proprietorial. The fact is that the phrase used in Persian – *Khalij-e Fars* – is composed of words of Arabic origin.

At the same time, as with the calendar reforms, there were progressive attempts to change the nomenclature of the country to reflect the nationalist mood better, restoring historical place names (imagined or otherwise). Perhaps the most striking change, at least as far as foreign observers were concerned, was the decision in 1934 to insist on the use of the name 'Iran' for the country, as opposed to 'Persia', a decision which caused some unusual consternation among members of the foreign diplomatic corps at the time, and which has been regularly misrepresented since as indicative of the malign influence of Nazi Germany and the growing obsession with 'Aryanism'.[4]

In the first instance, this was not a change in the name of the country, Iranians had been calling their country 'Iran' for centuries, as had been noted by a string of travellers and diplomatic officials. The insistence on 'Iran' as opposed to 'Persia' relied in part on the belief that the latter was too associated in the Western mind with decadence and decay, not associations they wanted made with the modern 'industrial' Iran. Moreover, while some Iranian diplomats in Germany appeared to have been taken in by the developments in the Third Reich, this was far from the first time that Iranian officials had requested the proper use of the country's name, having sent a similar missive in 1924 to the Turkish government (who had regularly referred to Iran as 'Ajam').[5] Even those diplomats in Germany who had been seduced by the idea that 'Aryanism' would provide an ethnic bond with resurgent Germany appeared to have been talking at cross purposes with the ideologues in the Third Reich, whose concept of 'Aryan' was not related to 'Iran'.[6]

This was not to deny the fact that some – even quite educated – Iranians were enamoured by what they considered to be a distinct racial heritage that distinguished them from Turks and Arabs (although that historical antipathy had no need to be painted in racial terms), but this was far from being the official ideology of the State. Despite subsequent allegations, Reza Shah had no truck with the indigenous Iranian Nazi sympathies (a party was formed in 1940), any more than he did with the Communist party, seeing them both as threats to his authority, and the fact that he thought Princess Fawzia of Egypt a suitable bride for his son and heir should put paid to any notions that he was wedded to an idea of Aryan purity.

These associations stuck to Reza Shah because he fitted the mould of the great dictators of the age and it was easy, if lazy, to draw parallels between him and Mussolini and Hitler, especially when it suited Allied propaganda as a justification for the occupation of Iran in the Second World War. But of course, his manner, which became more authoritarian and suspicious as time progressed, did not help. Similarly, those intellectuals who supported him in the early years either peeled themselves away in desperation as his manner grew more abrasive or accepted – and at time sought to excuse – that his approach to even desirable reforms was counter-productive.

His harsh treatment of the tribes, for example, which caused immense hardship, was widely criticized even if there were few disagreements with the fundamentals of the policy. Reza Shah felt that the notion of nomadic tribes was detrimental to Iran's image and wanted them settled. This was a matter of political control and administrative efficiency. It was much more difficult to tax nomads. But perhaps the most evocative and controversial policy of the period was the imposition of new dress codes, a development that was not quite as unusual as some have subsequently sought to portray.

The same ethos had driven the reforming policies of Meiji Japan, but, as with other policies, Reza Shah's motivations were different from those of his intellectual backers. They believed that dress reform would liberate Iranians and encourage them to think differently. Reza Shah saw the new clothes as a type of civilian uniform. Inspecting newly attired parliamentary deputies in 1935, Reza Shah expressed himself mightily satisfied: 'His Majesty expressed pleasure and remarked that if I had been there some years ago I should have noticed a great difference. Then all were attired in various garbs, there was no cohesion, no corporate feeling. On the 6th June last the members were all dressed alike, there was uniformity and discipline; that was what a Parliament should be.'[7]

The adoption of new dress codes was a methodical process, achieved incrementally, though occasionally prompted by whim and the need not to appear backward. It was the visit of the Afghan king and queen for instance, in 1928, which encouraged an acceleration in women's unveiling as the appearance of the unveiled queen of Afghanistan reminded Iranians that it was unseemly to appear to be behind the Afghan curve. Reza Shah nonetheless moved cautiously at first, simply relaxing the strict rules on the veiling of women.

The main opponents of dress reform were naturally the clerics, many of whom regarded the changes as sacrilege and the importation of impure Western customs. The 'Pahlavi cap', which was the first significant change imposed on men, approximated to the French kepi, appealing to the Shah's military sense of propriety. The clergy objected because the peak made it difficult, if not impossible, for the devout to perform their prayers – although here they clearly underestimated the ingenuity of the average Iranian who simply reversed the cap.

The Pahlavi cap, for all its military allusions and its attractiveness for the Shah, was in any case an interim reform and, in short order, the 'European' or 'International' hat was adopted, under the pretext that such headwear had been common in the Sasanian era and therefore was authentically Persian. The situation for women, of course, was considerably worse, not so much because everyone opposed unveiling – views tended to reflect the social class – but because, for all concerned, it involved adaptation and expense on a scale that many found prohibitive. If men had to find a new wardrobe, this was doubly more expensive for women, who in addition had to learn the new etiquette of behaviour in public.[8]

The imposition of new dress codes was never going to be smooth, hence the incremental and gradual nature of the change. But there was little doubt that those tasked with enforcing these new rules often acted aggressively against those who were deemed to have resisted. The clerics were naturally the single group most vehemently opposed to the changes and had managed to secure exemptions for themselves – ensuring, ironically, that they were the one group of people to be distinguished by their continued use of the turban and gown. Matters, however, came to a tragic end in Mashhad in 1935 in the infamous Goharshad Mosque incident, where protesters were fired upon by security forces.

Clerics had decided to preach against the dress reforms, condemning what was considered to be a process of Westernization. The local commander, watching the unrest unfold, panicked and opened fire with machine guns, resulting in some 18 fatalities and upwards of 50–60 wounded. Seemingly disturbed by the consequences of his own actions, the officer then withdrew and there was concern that his conscript troops could not be relied upon to hold firm. They were swiftly replaced by new troops who proceeded to make matters much worse, also opening fire with machine guns, killing a further 128 people and wounding up to 300.[9]

To say it was a catastrophe would be an understatement, but it was compounded by the fact that a delegation sent to the Shah to seek redress was dismissed. Reza Shah had little time for those he considered reactionary, but his manner was not calculated to reassure people, many of whom still held faith in the principle of the monarch as the 'father of the nation'. The administrator of the shrine, who was considered responsible, was swiftly arrested and executed but the events did not deter Reza Shah from pushing ahead with the legislation outlawing veiling in 1936.

Assessment

Reza Shah could never claim to be popular, and much of the enthusiasm that had greeted his arrival, especially among the intellectuals, had largely dissipated by the end of the 1930s. But then Reza Shah never really cared about popularity. What he craved was respect, and the nationalism he espoused and pursued, even if at times clumsy, enjoyed the support of much of the Iranian political elite. If they complained about his authoritarianism in private, they tended to parrot his lines in public.

There was little doubt that, in a very short space of time, the country was being transformed. Some of this was visual and symbolic, though there was much pride in the paraphernalia of the 'nation state': the flag, the anthems and the appeal to distinctly Persian forms. There was much criticism of his obsession with 'modern' town planning and the consequent destruction of traditional buildings. But it says much that the main thoroughfare still running north–south through Tehran is the boulevard he built (once Pahlavi Street, now Vali-Asr).

The development of transport infrastructure was impressive when you consider the terrain and the costs involved. There were 2,000 miles of roads, often in poor condition, in 1925. This had expanded to a network of some 14,000 miles by the end of his reign, much of it well maintained. His pride and joy was the development of a railway. It was modest by international standards, but an achievement when one considers the engineering required and the fact that the railway was funded through domestic taxation.

Critics argued that the north–south railway connecting Mazandaran in the Caspian to the oil fields in the south-west was constructed at the behest of the British, with an eye to supplying Russia in the Second World War. Quite apart from the degree of foresight this would have required (the project was inaugurated in 1927), the route of the railways was clearly dictated by Reza Shah's desire to connect his own (burgeoning) estates in Mazandaran to the rest of the Iranian plateau, as well as to obtain a means to shift troops swiftly south to the oil-rich regions, if required.

In many ways, the ability to connect the otherwise secluded Caspian provinces, shielded as they were by the Alborz mountain range, to the major cities of the plateau, including the capital Tehran, facilitated the development of a single Iranian market. It is indeed a testament to the ambitions and achievements of this period that the road from Tehran to Chalus on the Caspian was connected by a one-way single-lane tunnel through the mountains that was not made two-way until the late 1990s.

But there was much more. Healthcare was improved. A Pasteur Institute, modelled on its namesake in Paris, was founded in 1923 with a view to improving public health, while a veterinary bureau was established in 1925. A small medical school was established by 1930, and while most doctors were still trained abroad, the numbers grew, albeit slowly. By 1941, legislation was passed authorizing vaccination against a range of diseases. A national bank – Bank Melli – was established in 1928, and by 1931, with some reluctance, the British Imperial Bank of Persia lost its monopoly over the issuance of bank notes.

Education reform witnessed dramatic increases in numbers of students in both primary and tertiary education, with some 55,960 primary students in 1925 increasing to 287,245 by 1941. University students – taught in Iran – increased from 600 to 3,000 in the same period. These were in absolute terms modest figures – secondary school expansion was especially small, given the paucity of teachers – but this reflected, as noted above, the difficulties of starting a programme from scratch. The real explosion in student numbers would occur in the next decades, as teacher numbers reached a critical mass.

These tangible results meant that, for all his character flaws, Reza Shah remained respected, if not loved. While contemporaries attacked his growing paranoia and perceived avarice, perhaps the greatest criticism that could be levelled at Reza Shah was the incompleteness of his achievement. He had built and empowered the State but done little to balance that with an empowered and legally protected citizenry. The development of the modern State, a functioning bureaucracy with tax-raising powers and an army capable at the very least of local policing and the maintenance of order, gave Reza Shah a power and reach into Iranian society that few of his predecessors could imagine. But few could deny that, in a relatively short space of time, the foundations of the modern State had been laid.

As a British diplomat noted:

Oriental despots are never loved, and do not expect to be. As an oriental despot the Shah is probably above average in benevolence to the people at large . . . They are aware of his land and money grabbing propensity, but that is not a new characteristic among Persian noblemen; they are painfully aware of heavy taxation; they are probably less interested in the safety on the highways, which is one of the things that most strikes an European. But the Persians are, I believe, proud of what Reza has done for them.[10]

3

Oil and Nationalism
(1941–1953)

The last few years of Reza Shah's rule can best be described as tired. Progress was still being made in the development of the state but much of the energy of the earlier years was found wanting, and Reza Shah's focus turned to ensuring a smooth dynastic succession. Far from a sentimental person, Reza Shah occasionally betrayed a genuine affection for his son and heir, Mohammad Reza, which surprised courtiers more used to the Shah's brusque manner, even if he voiced doubts about his son's ability to rule. Reza Shah had dispatched his son to Switzerland for his education, convinced that Iran's rulers needed to be knowledgeable about the world. He was to find his son's sentimentality, expressive piety and superstition frustrating. On his son's return, he swiftly negotiated a marriage with the oldest of the current Middle Eastern dynasties, the Egyptian monarchy. It says something about the comparative state of affairs that Fawzia, the sister of King Farouk, found Tehran dreary and backward.

International affairs were soon to take a turn for the worst. The outbreak of war in 1939 and the fall of France in 1940 dramatically altered the geopolitical situation. Reza Shah was determined to keep Iran out of the war while maintaining cordial relations, as far as possible, with all parties. This was especially important as one of the problems faced by Iran was that some of its industrial purchases now came from countries under Nazi occupation. Moreover, there was a sizeable German expatriate community in Iran – far from unmanageable, but one that the British viewed with anxiety, not least because of the prospects for sabotage, but also for wider political mischief, as had been seen with the pro-German Rashid Ali coup in neighbouring Iraq.

Reza Shah had no sympathy with Nazism, even if some of his countrymen sympathized with Germany as the enemy of the two great imperial powers that had been squeezing Iran for the better part of a century. Unfortunately for Reza Shah, developments overtook him. The Germans had finally launched their invasion of the Soviet Union, driving far more rapidly towards Moscow than anyone had expected. The German drive southwards meanwhile, towards the oil fields of the Caucasus, raised real fears of a move towards Iran, not in strict military terms, but in terms of encouraging a German fifth column in Iran to take action.

Given the experience in the Great War, these fears were not wholly misplaced. Moreover, British oil interests in Iran were now emphatically a strategic asset on which much of Britain's war effort depended, and if the prospect of a military invasion was slight, it was not beyond the realms of possibility that, with airbases in the surrounding territories, Germany might be able to launch bombing campaigns on the refinery at Abadan.

In August 1941, the British and the Soviets took the fateful decision to invade and occupy Iran. There was an acute awareness, at least in British circles, about the dubious legality of what they were doing, and Churchill had privately noted that, while Britain had the justification, she did not have the right.[1] The Anglo-Soviet occupation had two main aims: the first was to protect vital oil supplies, but the other – no less significant – was to be able to use Iran as a land corridor for supplies to a weakened and vulnerable Soviet Union.

Having toyed with the idea of Reza Shah remaining, the Allies soon decided that his departure would be preferable. After some discussion and negotiation with the Iranian political elite, it was agreed that his 21-year-old son Mohammad Reza should succeed. This was a salutary reminder that, however ambivalent Iranians had become towards the person of Reza Shah, the Pahlavi project, itself an extension of the constitutionalist project, was not unpopular among the elite, and that, while they might disagree with the method, there was little dispute about the substance.

This became clear with subsequent developments. As politics slowly came back to life, politicians were quick to throw opprobrium on the departing Shah, not least for the woeful performance of the armed forces. Tribal leaders, who had been suppressed under Reza Shah and were now in open revolt, quickly

emerged to say that, had they not been forcibly settled, they would have been able to put up a much
more effective resistance. At the first realization that
the reaction to Reza Shah's departure might result in
an unwinding of his policies, not least those towards
the tribes, politicians swiftly hit the brakes.

The army was quickly rehabilitated, with the
humiliation of its rapid collapse being blamed on
Reza Shah's paranoia. It soon became apparent that
much else achieved under Reza Shah would remain in
place. But it was now imperative that the architecture
he had put in place – however imperfect – should
be developed. In this sense, the Allied Occupation
(1941–6) – the British and the Soviets were joined
by the Americans in 1942 – became an incubator for
political and social developments.

In the first place, this was the first time most
Iranians had encountered in any number foreigners
who were outside diplomatic or professional circles.
It is true that with commercial expansion, not least of
the Anglo-Iranian Oil Company, Iranians had encountered a wide range of professionals and, of course, the
Indian labour that had been brought into Abadan.
But never had so many Iranians encountered such a
breadth of foreigners, few of whom had any interest
whatsoever in Iran or the Iranians.

Moreover, this was an Allied Occupation in which
the three powers were in competition with each other
for influence, not simply the Anglo-Americans against
the Soviets, but the Americans against the British, as

the British were to discover when the Americans chose to bank with the National Bank of Iran, rather than the Imperial Bank of Persia. Their failure to anticipate this was reflective of a wider complacency that led inexorably to the winding down of operations and the departure of the Imperial Bank in 1949, following the end of the concessionary period.

The Soviets, meanwhile, energetically distributed wireless radio sets tuned into Radio Moscow, while the British and Americans sought to counter this propaganda with their own broadcasts. There was also another group of Europeans encountered by the Iranians in large numbers, and that was the Poles. Over 100,000 were now released from captivity in the Soviet Union and dispatched to Iran and then onwards – the menfolk at least – to be trained in the free Polish army.[2]

The Allies used Iran for the war effort, and all other things were secondary to that goal. Money was printed and spent which resulted in a rise in inflation with its associated hardships, but there was also investment in the necessary infrastructure to ensure that supplies could be delivered efficiently to the Soviet Union. The idea that Reza Shah's transport infrastructure was created with Allied needs in mind was negated by the reality that the network as it stood was not fit for this particular purpose.

The reinvigoration of politics was perhaps the single most important gain of the occupation. Reza Shah, for all his constitutional pretensions, had kept a tight lid on independent political activity, and once he was removed from the scene it was natural that politics would reflexively spring back into action. That is not to say that Iran was remotely 'democratic' in the commonly understood sense of the term. This was personality-led politics, in which established political figures set up parties and the machinery around them, including a supportive newspaper or two. (The one exception to this rule was the communist Tudeh Party.) Political life, for so long suppressed, now became volatile, with governments coming and going with alarming frequency. In the ten years following Reza Shah's abdication and exile (he was to die in South Africa in 1944), Iran had 17 prime ministers with the longest administration being 324 days.

The new monarch, Mohammad Reza Shah, found himself largely incidental to these political developments, though that was not for want of trying. Urged on by those who told him to emulate his father, he attempted to rehabilitate his father's reputation by emphasizing his singular role in the creation of modern Iran and downplaying allegations about his financial greed and amassing of land. Reza Shah's financial assets were to prove considerably less than many had suspected.[3] As for the extensive crown estates, Mohammad Reza Shah decided on a policy of redistribution of land, allowing the new king to present himself as an enlightened figure.

A failed assassination attempt,[4] allegedly by a member of the Tudeh Party (resulting in the party being outlawed), also served to boost popular sympathy for the young monarch and allowed him to pursue the crowning achievement of this process: the return of his father's body for a State funeral in 1949, along with the parliamentary dignity of his father being formally designated 'the Great', a development that was not without controversy.[5]

The Azerbaijan Crisis

The Allied powers had agreed that they would leave Iran no more than six months after the conclusion of the war. But as the Americans and British withdrew their forces, it was increasingly clear that Stalin was in no hurry. The Red Army remained in residence in north-western Iran, casting a protective and nurturing shield over separatist tendencies in both Iranian Azerbaijan and Kurdistan. These movements proclaimed autonomy from the central government and decried the centralization and 'Persianization' pursued by Reza Shah.

Despite their protestations, the fear among politicians in Tehran – which was not unreasonable – was that this was a dangerous stepping-stone towards separation: that Russia would exploit any weakness, as it had done many times previously, to incorporate the territories within its own Soviet Empire.

The Azerbaijan Crisis of 1946 has been described as the first confrontation of the Cold War, in which the Americans basically pushed back against Russian demands and Truman stood up to Stalin. But domestic politics proved an equally effective deterrent, highlighting both the skills and 'elasticity' of Iranian politicians. The Prime Minister Ahmad Qavam, an aristocrat and politician of the old school, who publicly proclaimed sympathies towards Russia, had argued that the way to dislodge Russia was to offer her an incentive, and the Russians had made clear that they were keen on an oil concession in the north to match that of the British in the south.

Qavam suggested that this was a very reasonable and real possibility, caveating his offer with the important point that parliament would need to ratify any agreement. He must have known, of course, that, given the rising nationalist sentiment of many deputies, this was unlikely to enjoy a smooth passage but, in any case, Stalin appears to have been convinced. It is also likely that Stalin, fatigued by war, had decided, in the face of probable Allied opposition to what he was doing, that Qavam offered a useful 'face-saving' way out of the crisis.

Soviet forces withdrew in anticipation of a deal which never materialized, due to parliamentary opposition. Qavam proclaimed himself stung by parliament's intransigence, but, with the Red Army out of Azerbaijan, the path was cleared for a re-occupation by the Iranian army by the end of that year. The architect of the re-occupation was General Ali Razmara, a product of the French military school at Saint-Cyr, who took care to ensure that the young Shah was credited with the operation. This was in itself a delicate political exercise, but it appeared to have satisfied the Shah and to have the requisite positive impact on his popularity.

Iranian nationalists drew a different lesson. They had witnessed first-hand their ability to rebuff the Soviet Union and now wondered whether they should not be turning their gaze southwards towards the vast Anglo-Iranian Oil Company.

Oil Crisis

As noted earlier, the Anglo-Iranian Oil Company (AIOC) had been the lucrative result of a concession awarded in 1901. The terms of the original concession had proved frustrating for Iranian governments – not least Reza Shah, who had sought to renegotiate it. The absence of meaningful progress led him to abrogate it altogether, forcing the parties to seek adjudication at the League of Nations. The Iranian position was that the concession had been reached with an 'illegitimate' government, insofar as it predated the Constitutional Revolution – but, more importantly, that times had changed. Had an agreement been negotiated now, it was argued, then a 50–50 partnership would have been likely. The British, for their part, given the investment they had made in the company and its refinery, naturally resisted any such move. The talks were on the verge of collapse, with the threat of a company withdrawal, when the chairman, Sir John Cadman, paid Reza Shah a visit. A compromise was abruptly reached. Neither side was willing to terminate the relationship, though nationalists lamented the fact that Reza Shah had apparently blinked first.

In the event, despite the criticism within Iran, Cadman privately noted that he felt he 'had been well and truly plucked'[6] by Reza Shah, in agreeing to a new concession which guaranteed a minimum income per year of £750,000 (irrespective of the economic circumstances), and royalties calculated not on profits but on 'physical volumes of oil and the financial distribution which the Company made to its shareholders'.[7] The territory of the concession was reduced by some 80 per cent, and promises were made that the company would seek to reduce the number of non-Iranian employees.

As the company grew, however, many of the issues that had frustrated Iranians were to return in a magnified form. In 1929, the company employed 15,245 people, almost doubling to 27,180 in 1930, and reaching 55,000 in 1949. The Company required, and acquired, more foreign labour, mainly from the Indian subcontinent, which appeared to run counter to the promises made in 1933.

But at the same time such exponential growth meant that the AIOC represented the first truly industrial development in Iran, accompanied by the development of an organized and increasingly politicized working class.[8] It should have come as no surprise that left-wing ideas were starting to spread, and the communist Tudeh Party – the first real political party in Iran – was well embedded. This latter development meant that the Company, never one to assume responsibility for the grievances that arose, tended to blame any and all labour activism on agitation by the Soviet Union.

There is little doubt that Stalin was not keen on giving the British a smooth ride, but much friction could have been avoided if the Company had been more proactive and progressive in its attitude to local needs. The Company repeatedly protested that it delivered a generous policy of benefits to its workers, but the truth was found to be somewhat at odds with its claims, and when a British Parliamentary delegation paid a visit in 1946, its findings were not complimentary: 'Here were to be seen Persian labour living in squalid conditions under tents, etc., and without doubt this was the worst place we visited from the point of view of social amenities.'[9]

In the 1940s, two other developments occurred that were to sow the seeds of further discord. The first was the appointment in 1941 of a new chairman, Sir William Fraser, against the advice of the Foreign Office, with one diplomat noting, 'The judgement of some other people who have seen more of him than I, is that he is not quite of the quality necessary for this immensely important British institution.'[10]

To this was added the realization that, as a result of increases in corporation tax during the war, the

Company was paying far more in tax to London than in royalties to Tehran. The incongruity naturally grated with Iranians, and if Reza Shah could dismiss political agitation, in the febrile atmosphere of the 1940s no government was strong enough to resist the intensely nationalist mood, certainly among the political class. Fraser and the Company Board meanwhile proved remarkably tone deaf to the problems emerging, soldiering on in the belief that international law would allow them to weather any local storm.

The British Labour government was much less sure, and, cognizant of the changing mood along with Britain's diminished stature in the world, the Foreign Secretary Ernest Bevin mused, as early as 1946, on the choppy waters that might lie ahead:

> Although we have a Socialist government in this country there is no reflection of that fact in the social conditions in connexion with this great oil production in Persia. On the other hand, what argument can I advance against anyone claiming the right to nationalize the resources of their country? We are doing the same thing here with our power in the shape of coal, electricity, railways, transport and steel. The Russians have overcome this difficulty by the Russian Government and the Persian government entering into a 50–50 company . . . The more I have studied the question the more I have come to the conclusion that instead of anything on the basis of royalties it would be preferable to examine the question whether

Great Britain and Persia should not now enter into an arrangement for a joint company on similar lines [to the Russian–Persian], and so establish the relationship between the Abadan Oilfield and the Persian government on a basis which is mutually advantageous . . . a more secure basis for our oil supplies by virtue of the fact that the Persian Government will be protecting its own property instead of that of a private company.[11]

The truth was that the post-war world was changing, new contracts were being negotiated, and the Company needed to show some flexibility and move with the times. The crisis which emerged over Iran's decision to nationalize the oil industry in 1951 might have been averted had those Company officials shown more foresight, and indeed listened to the advice of wider counsel in both the British and American governments. The problem with the American advice was that few British officials trusted it to be impartial and thought, with some justification, that it tended to encourage the Iranians to be more hard-line in their demands.

The Americans pursued a contradictory policy towards the British in the Middle East, at once seeking to accelerate the decline of the British Empire – with a keen eye on the spoils – while at the same time wanting to bolster Britain as a Cold War ally against the Soviet Union.[12] For the British government, AIOC was a commercial asset that allowed it to purchase oil in pounds sterling and avoid the vagaries of exchange rates. For the Americans, meanwhile, dominating the international oil markets and making sure that all commercial transactions were priced in dollars was an important ambition.

These conflicting interests aside, there was an awareness on the British part that a revised agreement needed to be reached with the Iranians, though the Company was reluctant to move towards a 50–50 arrangement which both Bevin and the Americans thought sensible. The Supplemental Agreement that was tabled in 1949 sought to increase revenues for Iran within the framework of the current arrangements, on the basis that it would guarantee income in bad years, which a 50–50 share agreement would not.

While there was as yet little support for outright nationalization, there was naturally a growing view that Iran should enjoy the same arrangement as other countries. A vocal minority in the parliament led by Dr Mohammad Mosaddeq, a veteran of the Constitutional Movement, who now headed the Special Oil Commission of the Iranian parliament, continued to agitate for full nationalization.

In 1950, as the crisis grew, the hero of the re-occupation of Azerbaijan, General Ali Razmara, was appointed Prime Minister. Razmara, largely overshadowed by Mohammad Mosaddeq, remains one of the most interesting people to have occupied the post. He immediately resigned his military commission and set to work trying to restore a measure of political stability to the country, including a plan to devolve power (if not authority) away from the centre and allow the provinces to have more control over local government. This was in many ways a reversion back to the original ideas of the Constitutional Revolution, which had eschewed the idea of a strong centralized state on the French model.

The other main issue in his in-tray was, of course, the oil crisis. News that Saudi Arabia was reaching a 50–50 agreement with Aramco appears to have finally convinced the Company to relent and, in early 1951, Razmara reached agreement on these grounds in principle, which he felt increasingly confident he could present to the parliament. Before he could do so, however, on 7 March he was assassinated while attending a memorial service at a mosque, for a recently deceased Ayatollah. The manner of his assassination and the fact that many parliamentary deputies seemed to rejoice in the news was a damning indictment of the febrile atmosphere caused by nationalism, but also did little to reassure the British that they had a reliable negotiating partner.

Among the parliamentarians, Razmara's assassination had a chilling effect. Nationalization was swiftly approved. After several months, and with some reluctance, the Shah called for the head of the Oil Commission, Dr Mohammad Mosaddeq, to take the helm. Since he had been so uncompromising in his demands for nationalization, many thought it right that he now take responsibility for the crisis they felt

he had done so much to fuel. Much to their surprise
– and that of the Shah – Mosaddeq, at the age of 69,
willingly took on the challenge.

Nationalization became a fact, and the Labour government found itself facing a crisis of emulation it
would rather have avoided. The details of the ensuing
crisis over the next two years need not preoccupy us
here, but it was clear that, with the frame of reference
now changed, attempts to find a compromise became
even more difficult than before. If, prior to 1951, the
Iranians had approached the matter as one of politics
and principle, and the British from the perspective of
legal and commercial technicalities, now the tables
were turned.

For the Iranians, the principle had been achieved;
it was now a matter of getting it accepted and ironing
out the details of how it might work. For the British,
on the other hand, this blow beneath the imperial
belt was a matter of principle that had to be resisted.
British opinion veered at times towards the hysterical
in their depictions of the Iranian position, in part to
dislodge the Americans from what they considered to
be a louche position that had encouraged the Iranians
to nationalize in the first place.

The Americans, meanwhile, played the anti-
imperial role, with an eye to them seizing the initiative
in Iran. The Iranians felt they could exploit this
difference between the two wartime allies to their
advantage, while the British, determined to protect
this most important of overseas assets, closed ranks

(misgivings about the Company were now set aside) and increasingly stressed the Cold War frame of reference with the Americans, in an effort to excite them out of what they considered to be a dangerous political stupor.

The Americans felt the communist threat to be exaggerated, but that did not mean they were oblivious to it. Far from it. These were the days of the McCarthyite hearings and the Korean War, after all, so it was more a question of tactics than strategy, and the Iranians were unwise not to see this broader canvas. It is, as such, no doubt true that the focus was on the control of oil, but that control mattered because of wider Cold War anxieties.

At the same time, the mind-set that concluded that the 'intransigent' Mosaddeq might need to be replaced in favour of a more compliant government was arguably less Cold War and more Second World War, given the military experience of most of the operatives subsequently involved and the long shadow cast by the war on those ultimately taking the political decisions. That the tragedy which unfolded in August 1953 might have been avoided was voiced early by Mosaddeq, in December 1951, when he opined in the parliament that nationalization was not an inevitability – a statement that surprised some of his colleagues – and that, had the British offered a 50–50 agreement much earlier, the current impasse might have been avoided.[13] Mosaddeq the politician lamented the quagmire that developed.

His ambitions had been to redefine the relationship with Britain as a means of pursuing the constitutional aims of the Revolution of 1906. By empowering Iranians through a successful – if limited – confrontation with Britain, all sorts of new political vistas might be opened.[14] Unfortunately, the romantic got the better of the politician and Mosaddeq soon realized that anything less than nationalization would not deliver, forcing him down a path that resulted in a confrontation with Britain that was anything but limited. Britain increasingly saw the dispute as existential to her continued Great Power status and was not willing to yield.

While Britain engaged in contingency planning, Mosaddeq weakened his own position by taking increasingly unconstitutional measures to shore up his government, resulting in many allies – not least the versatile Ayatollah Kashani, important for control of the streets – withdrawing their support. Ironically, Mosaddeq's anxiety about a possible coup encouraged him down avenues that made a coup more possible, not least with his decision to circumvent the parliament, reduce the powers of the Shah and curtail the pensions and prerogatives of retired officers.[15]

By 1952, continued friction with Britain, resulting from not unjustifiable claims of political interference, led to the breaking of diplomatic relations and the closure of the British Embassy. This meant that any coup planning now resided with the United States. Meanwhile, the election of Eisenhower in November

1952 resulted in a new dynamic in the United States, and not least in the relationship with Britain, where Churchill had been returned to Downing Street in late 1951. Enthusiasm for a coup was still, however, muted, and attempts to find a mutually satisfactory resolution were pursued into 1953.

Only once the Americans felt they had exhausted all avenues were plans enacted in late spring, with networks established to contend with a Soviet invasion being mobilized to deal with Mosaddeq. The plan, which relied on the constitutional prerogative of the Shah to dismiss his Prime Minister, faced a final hurdle when it became quite clear that the Shah himself was not at all keen on the idea, aware of the popularity that Mosaddeq retained among wide swathes of the population. Ultimately, familial pressure appears to have done the trick and officers were dispatched to the prime ministerial residence with the note of dismissal.

Mosaddeq reacted with remarkable calm, bordering on complacency, and his failure to acknowledge the dismissal confounded the plotters. Once word got out, crowds poured out in support of the Prime Minister. The Shah immediately considered that discretion was the better part of valour and decided to depart on a 'holiday' abroad. It appeared that the coup had failed, and it fell to operatives on the ground, not least the CIA's Kermit Roosevelt, to have another go. This time the orchestration worked. Mosaddeq found himself out-manoeuvred and, without the necessary allies, ended up barely escaping following a shoot-out between the rival parties at his residence. The Shah, meanwhile, hearing the news of Mosaddeq's deposition while in Rome, flew back elated by the realization – somewhat misplaced – that his people really did 'love' him after all.[16]

The reality was more sanguine. Faced with the continuing crisis, and an economy in disarray, Iranians were increasingly open to the idea of change. Mosaddeq enjoyed a continuing popularity, which was one reason why the Shah remained reluctant to act, but key parts of society were becoming disillusioned with the Prime Minister, who seemed to offer no solutions. They rallied round the institution, if not the person, of the monarchy. Whether these forces would have eventually led to Mosaddeq's downfall, we will never know because the decision was made in Washington and London to accelerate developments, leaving an exceptionally bad taste among many Iranians to this day.

4

The 'White' Revolution (1954–1977)

For many nationalist Iranians, a direct line can be traced from the coup of 1953 to the eventual overthrow of the Shah in 1979. One leads inexorably to the other. Mohammad Reza Shah, having been restored to the throne through foreign intervention, forfeited his legitimacy and struggled consequently to stabilize his rule. For those of an Islamist bent, the origins of the Revolution of 1979 can be traced to the religiously inspired uprisings of 1963 against the Shah's reforms, known as the White Revolution. Both narratives contain a grain of truth, but both are also heavily deterministic in their reading of Iranian history, reading backwards from the traumatic events of 1979 to lend those events an air of inevitability and provenance. The truth is that the quarter-century following the coup in 1953 was a period of enormous socio-economic change and opportunity. Ultimately it was decisions made by the Shah rather than faceless structures that would determine the fate of himself, his dynasty and the country.

Mohammad Reza Shah returned to Iran thrilled in the belief that his people did after all hold him in some affection. As was soon to become apparent, this was to prove a dangerous misreading of the situation.

Few people, outside hardcore royalists, held the person of the Shah in any esteem, even if many considered the institution of monarchy essential to the stability and progress of the country. On the contrary, many viewed the Shah as well-meaning but frivolous, and that included many of his Anglo-American backers. The British had never been overwhelmed by the Shah and, for all their disdain for his father, at least regarded Reza Shah as a man of decision. Mohammad Reza Shah on the other hand, as the events of August 1953 revealed, seemed to be wracked by indecision and self-doubt. The Americans were prepared to give the Shah the benefit of the doubt but were soon to find themselves frustrated.

As the British had foreseen, the real beneficiaries of the coup were the Americans. A new oil consortium was negotiated in 1954, which saw Anglo-Iranian, now renamed British Petroleum, take a 40 per cent share, and another 40% taken up by American oil companies. The new Prime Minister, General Zahedi, a relative of Mosaddeq who had served as a minister in one of his cabinets, was a strong military man of the type favoured by the United States. Ironically, the British had arrested him for Nazi sympathies during the war, but now he basked in an all too short glory as he soon found his sovereign less willing to share the spoils than he had thought. Indeed, few learned the lessons of Razmara – that, for all one might achieve, wisdom dictated that the bulk of the credit be allocated to a shah who remained jealous of his prerogatives.

The Shah, meanwhile, keen to take political centre stage, was acutely aware of the limitations of his power, and as such seemed averse to taking responsibility, lest his power weaken further. A particularly egregious example of this occurred in 1955, when a pogrom was launched against the Bahais. The Shah privately expressed regret for what had happened, but British diplomats were scathing about his inactivity, drawing a stark and unfavourable comparison with his father. A number speculated that he had been blackmailed on account of his playboy lifestyle. However, a more convincing argument can be made for the fact that this was payback for clerical support during the coup. Whatever the reality, the lack of progress with regard to political and economic development was to prove irksome for the Americans, who found the Shah's continued demands for military aid and support misplaced.

That said, the Americans were only too keen to ensure that the Shah's position was stabilized and secure against the possibility of political and social turmoil, to say nothing of the fear of Soviet intervention. Whatever reservations there might have been about developing the military and security apparatus, these were, initially at least, dismissed in light of wider Cold War anxieties, which the Shah was only too keen to play on. One of the more notorious developments was that of the security services known by the Persian acronym SAVAK. SAVAK had been founded following the termination of the military government in Tehran in 1957. General Bakhtiar, the military governor who would then go on to become the first head of SAVAK, gained a reputation for brutality and the effective reintroduction of torture to terrorize political opponents.[1]

It remains one of the great paradoxes of modern Iranian history that the systematic reintroduction of torture should have occurred in the rule of the first Iranian monarch to have been Western-educated and to have espoused Western sensibilities. It never reached the scale of the post-revolutionary period, but its presence was to prove a scarring blight on Mohammad Reza Shah's reign.

Some might excuse such excesses if the reform of Iran's political economy carried on apace but, by the end of the 1950s, there was little sign of progress, not least because so much of the aid being afforded to Iran was being directed to the military-security apparatus. This was a concern shared by one of the Shah's leading economic officials, Abolhasan Ebtehaj, the man who had emerged from the British Imperial Bank of Persia to bring his former employer – the Imperial Bank – to heel, and was now heading up the Plan and Budget Organization, an institution established in 1949 to guide the country through managed development. Ebtehaj repeatedly clashed with the Shah over the level of military expenditure, arguing that the proper way to immunize the country against a communist takeover was to develop it economically, with proper welfare for all. The communist threat came from within not without, and there was no point having a powerful military if the State was effectively built on sand. Many Americans sympathized with this view, even as the Shah pressed for further military aid.

By the end of the decade, rumours circulated that the Americans had become so frustrated that they had considered launching another coup to sideline, if not remove, the Shah. In the event, with the election of the Democratic administration of Kennedy, the Shah was encouraged – albeit with some reluctance – to appoint the former ambassador to the United States, Dr Ali Amini, to the position of Prime Minister, with the avowed intention of launching a deep reform of the State. The West had watched with some trepidation the fate of the Iraqi monarchy in 1958, and the Iranians had likewise viewed with some anxiety the military coup in Turkey which had occurred in 1960.

The view had gathered pace that some radical medicine needed to be applied to Iran if it was to avoid the same fate, and some courtiers had argued that the best way to get the Shah on board was to get him to lead this change, heading a 'white', bloodless revolution from above. The idea of a revolutionary monarchy did not appeal to the Shah. In an interview in 1958, a journalist noted that, 'He [the Shah] often grew impatient when American diplomats urged him to modernize at a pace faster than his careful crawl. "I can start a revolution for you", he apparently told an American diplomat, "but you won't like the end result."'[2]

The Shah's lack of enthusiasm for the project resulted in attention being refocused on Amini, who soon launched what he described as a 'white revolution': a comprehensive transformation of the country's socio-economic relations, largely through the imposition of a vast land reform programme, transferring land to and empowering peasants. The whole process, well intentioned as it was, had the air of a social science thesis about it, as the practical consequences rarely matched the theoretical ambitions.

The idea was to transform Iran's 'feudal' relations, but for some this was seen as a political move to disenfranchise the aristocracy with a view to destabilizing the State, not an exercise in social and economic regeneration. Some of these views undoubtedly reflected the vested interests under threat, but there was little doubt that Amini's Minister for Agriculture, Hasan Arsanjani, harboured radical thoughts about the future of the monarchy and regarded the weakening of the aristocracy as an important means to a wider end.[3] Be that as it may, Amini's administration was not strong enough to weather the storm ahead. Opposed domestically by a range of opponents, including the clerical classes (themselves occasionally landowners), Amini found his American supporters less than willing to provide him with the funds necessary to sustain his government.

Meanwhile, the Shah, now persuaded of the merits of this 'white revolution', decided he should indeed take the lead and launch *the* White Revolution, with a definitive referendum – securing an impressive '99 per cent' of the vote – inaugurating six key reforms of the State: land reform, nationalization of the forests, profit sharing for industrial workers, sale of State factories, votes for women, and the establishment of a literacy corps with the aim of sending teachers into rural areas. To these six points would be added a further six, reaching a total of seventeen policies by 1976. This would also in time be renamed the 'Shah–people revolution', just so that no one had any doubt of the authorship. In time he would define his aim as a 'Great Civilization', where all Iranians would receive the material benefits of a bountiful State from the cradle to the grave.

If there had been problems with land reform before, these now became acute, and even American advisors commented that their ideas for economic regeneration were largely being transplanted by the Shah's ambitions to consolidate his power. Indeed, the Shah appeared to have been persuaded to lead this new revolution on the basis that it would establish his monarchy on what amounted to Bonapartist principles, circumventing the aristocracy and talking straight to the people, empowered and ever grateful to the Shah for their new status as landowners.

More than abolishing 'feudalism', the Shah acted as if he had abolished serfdom, but, as with all things, one size did not fit all. The patchwork quilt that made up modern Iran was ill suited to the sort of rationalization being envisaged here. It was one thing to centralize the State as his father had done – though even here many had thought Reza Shah had gone too far – but standardizing society was an altogether different prospect, especially as the State became increasingly powerful through new technologies and oil wealth.

There were two ways in which land reform did not deliver on its promise. The first, as foreign advisors noted, was the fact that many of the landholdings were far too small to be economically viable, with the consequence that the new owners simply sold them back for cash and then moved to the cities. These arguably would have been the labour for new industries, had these materialized in sufficient numbers. The reality was that many became part of the new lumpenproletariat, disenfranchised, and lost in the new Iran.

The second flaw was more subtle. The political emasculation of the aristocracy was, on the face of it, regarded as a progressive move towards a more equal society. Setting aside its unequal application – some very large landowners remained – it removed at a stroke a key element in the Iranian social structure which served to mediate both economic and political relations.

Traditionally, if a worker had a need or a complaint they would go to their local landlord. If they needed extra tools to work their land, they could turn to their landlord, who may or may not provide them. But the relationship was immediate and personal. With this connection removed, workers now had to apply to the Ministry of Agriculture to get their needs attended to. Quite apart from requiring a degree of literacy and bureaucratic fluency, many complained that the young technocrats who were frequently sent knew little about local conditions and the practicalities of farming.

For the Shah, of course, the absence of this mediating class removed a key element that could explain and translate the programme of modernization, and that could moderate, through patronage, those radicals (especially among the clergy) who might oppose such a programme, and, perhaps most seriously, that served as a shield against direct criticism of the Shah and the monarchy. In time, those aristocrats who felt that they had been unfairly stripped of their patrimony would turn their ire on the Americans they felt had been the inspiration for it.

One of the influences on the programme of modernization was held to be Samuel Huntington, whose book *Political Order in Changing Societies* was deemed to have outlined the authoritarian programme pursued by the Shah. Quite apart from the fact that the book was published in 1968, the main thesis of the book appears to have been misunderstood by its Iranian critics. Huntington was in fact criticizing the social scientific approaches to modernization which apparently had been adopted by the Shah and his legion of US-educated technocrats, which regarded economic development as the *sine qua non* of progress.

Since the Americans had never had to develop political institutions, having inherited them from Great Britain, their focus had settled on economic development as the keystone for political progress, which would surely follow as night follows day.[4] Consequently, there was no need to look at institution building, the legal and political architecture within which economic development might flourish. This was, in time, to prove a dangerous omission and one that flatly contradicted the approach developed in the Constitutional Revolution and its aftermath. Those who hoped and expected that Mohammad Reza Shah would complete the process begun by his father were to be sorely disappointed.

The Red and the Black

A good example occurred soon after the launch of the White Revolution, with the discussions about implementing the Status of Forces Agreement (SOFA) granting extra-territorial legal rights to American personnel working in Iran. In 1964, as a matter of routine, the US State Department requested that the Iranian government accept the SOFA for the protection of US diplomatic personnel working in Iran. This was not simply a matter of diplomatic immunity, but an agreement, reached with many other US allies, that would allow any American government employee (broadly defined) and their dependants to be tried in a US court for any crime committed in Iran. This was not an unusual request for the United States, but the definition of those who were included was deemed quite broad and taken by many in Iran as an indication of their lack of confidence in the Iranian legal system – not, as it happened, an unreasonable assumption.

The Americans had suggested that a bilateral agreement could be reached between the governments, minimizing publicity and any fallout that might accrue. The Prime Minister Ali Mansur, however, decided that such were the sensitivities that only open ratification in parliament would do. As the Americans suspected, this only created further turmoil. Iranian nationalists were aghast at the prospect of a return to the 'capitulations', as they saw it, abolished with such aplomb by Reza Shah in 1927. Mohammad Reza Shah's decision to accept the US request seemed to be a betrayal of his father's promise. There was, to be sure, more politics than reality in all this, but the politics was real enough and the distress vocal. Outside parliament, among the most vocal critics was a relatively young firebrand cleric by the name of Ruhollah Khomeini.

Khomeini had come to prominence criticizing the principles of the White Revolution, notably the land reform and votes for women. Protests that had been inspired by his rhetoric – which his acolytes were to regard as the start of the Islamic awakening that led ultimately to revolution in 1979 – were ruthlessly suppressed, and Khomeini himself was kept under house arrest in Qom for six months. When, a year later, news of the new agreement came to light, Khomeini was even less subtle in his criticism, arguing that 'they have reduced the Iranian people to a level lower than that of an American dog'. If an Iranian ran over an American dog, he would be subject to prosecution, but the same would not be true if 'an American cook' ran over the Shah. Rhetoric of this nature marked Khomeini out to be a cleric with a political touch. These were not the finer points of theology he was discussing, but highly pointed political remarks.

As the Shah was persuaded to send Khomeini into exile – he was rapidly elevated to Ayatollah (a title accorded to the most senior religious jurists) to avoid the indignity of arrest – he might have reflected on earlier prevarications that had provided Khomeini with an opportunity to seize the mantle of clerical leadership.

In 1961, the recognized leader of the clerical hierarchy, Ayatollah Boroujerdi, a dedicated quietist (non-political) cleric of the old school, had died. The Shah had visited him on his death bed. Tradition dictated that the Shah should acknowledge a successor, who, in the informal hierarchy that existed, would nonetheless fulfil a leadership role. The Shah demurred, in the belief that leaving this 'position' vacant would remove the possibility of anyone being a thorn in his side. It was a decision he would come to rue.

Having been a reluctant revolutionary, the Shah was now impatient for change and increasingly irritated by anyone who might voice an alternative opinion. This was not simply revolutionary socialists or religious reactionaries (defined by the Shah as the 'Red and the Black'), but increasingly the secular nationalists who felt the Shah's enthusiasm for economic growth was coming at the expense of meaningful political development. Not an especially violent man, he nonetheless enjoyed cultivating an image of ruthlessness that disguised weaknesses in character that foreign observers had noted in 1953. The suppression of the protests in 1963, for example, were initiated by his Prime Minister, Asadollah Alam (later to become a highly influential Minister of Court).

Indeed, the impatience to pursue his 'mission' meant that he often overlooked matters of process and government that provided important checks on the excesses of power. This was particularly egregious where officials committed these excesses, and one of the peculiarities of the rule of the cosmopolitan and European-educated Mohammad Reza Shah was – as noted earlier – that the torture of political prisoners returned with a vengeance.[5] It has been suggested that the Shah was trying to impress his American allies with his anti-communist credentials, but the fact that these activities took place at all was a serious indictment of the new Shah's rule.

At the same time, when confronted by the realities of punishment, the Shah was quick to forgive and, as he pointed out, while he could not forgive those

who had betrayed their country, he forgave all those
who had sought to assassinate him (there were at least
two serious attempts). The Shah was undoubtedly an
autocrat. He had little time for what people generally
understood as democracy. But he was an ambivalent
dictator, and ultimately these contradictions in his
character would be his undoing.

For the present, however, the future appeared
bright. The opposition had been dismissed, marginal-
ized or sent into exile, the White Revolution had been
launched with great fanfare and apparent approval,
and the promised land beckoned. The decade from
1963 proved to be boon years for the economic development of Iran. Building on the foundations laid by
the Shah's father, the economy grew by an average
of 10 per cent per annum, leading some observers
to conclude that Iran was to be the new Japan and
the economic engine of the Middle East. This growth
was all the more impressive as oil revenue was yet
to make a serious impact on the country's finances,
averaging around $1 billion per year during the
decade.

As such, it supported growth but did not warp it,
even if the revenue helped to disguise some of the
anomalies that were emerging. Indications of a social
and economic transformation were already apparent
at the beginning of the decade as student numbers
grew, travel increased and means of communication
developed. In 1940, there were an estimated 100,000
radio sets in the country. By the early 1960s, this

had increased tenfold. But more impressive was the adoption of the television set, with some 67,000 sets in 1962 reaching an audience of some 670,000, 'an audience far exceeding the total number of readers of newspapers and magazines'.[6]

By the end of the decade, in 1967, the Shah finally felt confident enough to hold a coronation ceremony. But his real ambition was to hold a magnificent celebration of monarchy itself by commemorating the 2,500th anniversary of the foundation of the Persian Empire by Cyrus the Great in 559 BC, a celebration that was now, for largely logistical reasons, to be held in October 1971. This was meant to be a celebration of Persian (imperial) culture, though the focus was clearly on the idea of monarchy and the person of Cyrus the Great, a historical figure unfamiliar to most Iranians until the archaeological investigations of the nineteenth century.

Cyrus had liberated the Jews from Babylon: he was the great emancipator. It was not hard to see what drew the Shah to the figure of Cyrus, and he clearly identified with him. This was a step change from the traditional – mythological and legendary – history of pre-Islamic Iran that most Iranians understood from the poetic epic the *Shahnameh* or *Book of Kings*, and Mohammad Reza Shah's relegation of the latter in favour of his affectation for Cyrus the Great was seen by some as favouring Western readings of Persia over indigenous narratives of Iran. At the very least, most Iranians did not share the Shah's emotional bond to the ancient king, and found his affectation difficult to digest.

Many became highly critical of the reputed cost of the collective events, along with the tight security surrounding them. Much to the Shah's consternation, far from being a celebration of Iranian culture, it became a critique of Pahlavi decadence and shone an awkward light on the Shah's disdain for democratic norms.[7] These two themes were to become staples of foreign correspondents' questioning going forward, and were indeed to receive something of a boost following the Shah's next move.

Realizing the Great Civilization

In 1973, the Yom Kippur War led to an Arab oil boycott, which resulted in a quadrupling of the oil price that sent the Western world into recession. It was a significant shock to the Western system. The Shah for his part did not partake in the boycott, and continued to sell oil, while at the same time watching, listening and learning. By December of that year, he had decided to make his move.

The Shah had told his economic planners that they could expect a significant injection of cash and that their plans for the fifth five-year plan might have to be revised. The previous plan had seen some $7 billion of oil revenue injected into the economy over the five-year period, and the next plan envisaged $21 billion of oil investment. Economists at the Plan and

Budget Organization felt this was a level of investment which the Iranian economy could digest without over-inflating.

The Shah, impatient as ever, was keen to accelerate this growth. Some have suggested that this was a consequence of a recent diagnosis he had received of cancer, and that his impending mortality had focused his mind even further. But the evidence does not support this argument.[8] In any case, watching the response to the Arab boycott, the Shah decided to make an announcement of his own in which he declared a further quadrupling of the oil price, from the $3 it had reached that October to $11. At a stroke, the Shah delivered a further $70 bn of oil revenue to be injected into the economy.

December 1973 marks the high-water mark of the Shah's reign but, riding the crest of the wave, the Shah seemed acutely unaware of the dangers he now faced. The West, for their part, having contended with the Arab boycott, now faced the reality that their erstwhile ally was making life even more difficult. They rushed to adjust to new realities by engaging with the new 'Emperor of Oil', while somewhat resentful at the pain he had inflicted. The Shah, basking in the reflected glory of his economic triumph – the declaration also marked the moment Iran took full control of her oil resources, some twenty years after the coup against Mosaddeq – now failed to see the limits of the possible and went on what might best be termed a mad dash for growth, in spite of the advice

of his officials. They warned him that the economy
would soon overheat, leading to inflation and – in
the absence of clear legal and regulatory institutions
– corruption. The weaknesses of economic growth
absent a political framework may have been disguised
by modest oil revenues, but they would be exposed
by enormous revenues.

In the immediate term, though, everything seemed
positively rosy. If human rights organizations griped,
Western governments competed for attention and
money, setting aside any aspirations to an ethical
foreign policy in the interests of economic salvation.
More worryingly, Western diplomats who might
have spoken truth to power (in the main, British and
American) frequently self-censored to avoid incur-
ring the Shah's wrath, and later, with vast contracts
at stake, refused to conclude that anything but continued progress could result from the Shah's policies.

On many different levels, the Shah's economic
achievements were dramatic, but the heavy injection
of capital now served to warp the reality of growth,
such that in 1975 the Iranian government boasted
of 41 per cent annual growth, a figure so astonishing that only the truly credulous can have believed it
was an accurate reflection – or, indeed, remotely sustainable.[9] These figures, of course, reflected the huge
injection of oil revenue in an economy that was not
yet large enough to sustain it. It led to rampant inflation, supply tailbacks, a huge increase in imports and,
above all, corruption on a scale that was no longer

tolerable. Kickbacks had always been a feature of the Iranian economy, formal or otherwise, but the scale was now proving embarrassing, and the disparities in wealth emerging were so stark that anyone concerned with social stability would be worried.

For the Shah, however, these problems were transitory, necessary costs that had to be borne en route to the Great Civilization, his ambitious if somewhat vague plans for a cradle-to-grave welfare state, spiritually bound to the principle of *his* monarchy. Indeed, far from using the economic advantages he had garnered to begin a process of political reform and liberalization, the Shah was indignant when criticized by Western reporters about the absence of political freedoms, denying that Iranians were remotely interested in 'Western-style' democracy, and claiming that 'Iranian' democracy, as he saw it, was much more functional and suited to Iran, and that the West – and Britain, in particular – might take some lessons from his achievement.

As hubristic as these statements appeared to many, there were a good few Western politicians who fawned uncritically over the economic achievements on show, and fed the Shah's ego. In a now famous interview with Peter Snow, the Shah lambasted the laziness of British workers while barely disguising his glee at the estimates that had been made about Iranian economic growth: 'In 25 years Iran will be one of the world's five flourishing and prosperous nations . . . I think that in 10 years' time our country will be as you are now. I am not the only one who says this but, according to others, during the coming 25 years Iran will become one of the five most flourishing and prosperous nations of the world.'[10]

With the benefit of hindsight, such claims seem wildly out of place but, as the Shah noted, these were assessments being made by others, which served to validate his own confidence. Few were willing to dig deeper behind the statistics and, much as with China today, the focus lay almost exclusively on the extraordinary growth and potential that Iran enjoyed. It had abundant reserves of oil, and while the Shah noted with some reason that these were finite, Iran also enjoyed some of the largest natural gas reserves in the world, much of which remained untouched.

On top of that, the Shah enthusiastically endorsed and promoted an indigenous nuclear industry, with the emphasis on the latter. Iranians complained that they had been late to the development of an oil industry and that industrial capacity lay largely in the hands of the West. It would not make the same mistake again with regard to nuclear power, and would add to that capacity by exploring the options for solar power, a concept so innovative at the time that Khomeini would later mock the Shah for feeding his people fantasies.

Hubris

So confident did the Shah become that he completely lost sight of what many of his supporters thought the White Revolution had been about – the political development of the country. For his overseas backers, notably the Americans, that would come in good time; for his Iranian supporters, that time always seemed to be just over an ever-receding horizon.

Matters took a distinct turn for the worse when the Shah, frustrated at the theatrical farce of the two-party system he oversaw – a consequence in the main of his inability to allow them to operate – decided, by edict, to turn Iran into a one-party state, by establishing the Rastakhiz (Resurrection) Party. This would have two wings, which would help to incubate both ideas and leaders within a controlled frame of reference. The perverseness of this move was compounded by the announcement that all patriotic Iranians would clearly join the party, and that those who did not were clearly not patriotic and should get their passports and leave.

This comment was all the more astonishing for its flippancy. No one really believed they would have to leave the country, but the insult added to injury was acute and, in many ways, more resented than the establishment of the one-party state. The Shah was alienating his natural constituencies. The landowning elite had never been reconciled to the loss of their lands. Now the professional elite, overwhelmingly nationalist in sentiment, were offended by the demand to join a party they found ridiculous.

It only remained for the Shah to offend the clerical classes, never a group that were burdened with a sense of loyalty to him. Many remained quietist and avoided politics except in the most exceptional circumstances, and, even then, the comments were at best obtuse. But younger clerics, frustrated with what they saw as apathy, turned increasingly to the polemical Khomeini, now railing against the Shah from his exile in Iraq.

Khomeini, never one for theological niceties and viewed with some scepticism by his peers, seized the mantle of political leadership among the clerical hierarchy with a vengeance, giving a series of controversial lectures in 1970 under the rubric of 'Islamic Government', in which he articulated a system of government around the rule of the Guardianship of the Jurist.

Khomeini, long estranged from the idea of monarchy, took Shia political ideas to their logical conclusion by arguing that not only were all temporal governments illegitimate in the absence of the Hidden Imam (who, Iran's Shias believed, would return at the end of time), but that the only legitimate government in the meantime was one run by his theological representatives, the Jurists, of whom one would be selected as the Supreme Jurist and leader. This was not a radical idea – the roots of this sort of thinking were evident in the historical record, but to state it as he had was a radical departure, and many of his peers dismissed it as impractical nonsense that would only result in the ruination of Islam.

For many young clerics, along with other radical idealists – especially among the young, educated on an unprecedented scale yet denied a political voice – Khomeini's ideas were just the tonic, a return to authenticity for a society that seemed culturally adrift and over-enthused with all things Western. The idea that Iran had become 'West-toxicated' (*gharbzadeh*) had been popularized by the left-wing intellectual and writer Jalal Ale Ahmad in his eponymous book (*Gharbzadeh* (West-toxication)) who had himself taken the idea from a right-wing thinker Ahmad Fardid, whose influences included the German philosopher Heidegger. Khomeini was clearly familiar with the book and, in showing a modest interest in philosophy, further ingratiated himself with the left-wing intellectuals who were populating the dissident landscape.

For the Shah, his great fear continued to be the potential alliance between Red revolution and Black reaction. And while the security services had kept a close eye on the Left, the consensus was that the clergy would instinctively support the monarchy against a possible communist takeover, much as they appear to have done in 1953. So, the clerical hierarchy, while monitored, were never suppressed, mosques remained open and spirituality encouraged.

One speaker popular with the young, Ali Shariati, who preached a curious mix of Marxism and revolutionary Shiism, just the sort of combination that should have raised concerns in government circles, was at once indulged and harassed, according to the political mood. Shariati's ideas were not deep, but they were popular, and he was tolerated as long as it was felt his words added to the sum total of anti-communist spirituality. Similarly, the Shah made a great play of his own faith and kept up a steady investment in religious institutions, including various seminaries that enjoyed government largesse.

Then, in 1976, the Shah abruptly decided that his people had tired of the calendar in use since his father's reforms in 1924, which had been dated from the Prophet Muhammad's migration to Medina in 622, and instead should use an 'Imperial' calendar dated from the accession of Cyrus the Great in 559 BC. Overnight in March 1976, Iranians found themselves living not in 1355 but in 2535. It would be churlish to suggest that everyone detested it – quite a few enjoyed the imperial allusions. But one group – the clerics – reviled it, and some argued that this proved the Shah wanted to replace Islam with the ancient faith of Iran, Zoroastrianism.

Nothing could be further from the truth, but the Shah seemed blithely oblivious to criticism of any kind, impatiently dismissing it as irrelevant. As one apocryphal story has it, when the Shah asked a courtier what the difference was between him and his father, the courtier boldly answered that everyone feared telling his father a lie, but everyone feared telling him the truth. The Shah soldiered on, convinced that his Great Civilization was just around the corner.

5

Revolution and War
(1978–1988)

The French historian Alexis de Tocqueville famously wrote, in his study of the *Ancien Regime and the French Revolution*, that 'it is not always in going from bad to worse that one falls into revolution. It more often happens that a people who have borne without complaint, as if they did not feel them, the most burdensome laws, reject them violently once their weight is lightened.'[1] Tocqueville has proved a popular writer in Iran, in part because his analysis of the *ancien régime* and the reasons for its fall tends to mirror that of the Shah's regime. But also, interestingly, because Iran's new revolutionaries, for all their talk of Islam, tended to model themselves on the French Revolution, for which they have held an almost reverential adulation. This reflected the fact that many of the intellectuals who informed the new constitution were francophone, but also that the student body that did so much to drive the protests saw themselves as heirs of both 1968 and 1789. The parallels, which were often ill fitting, stretched to both the ad hoc 'komitehs' (committees) that were established to keep order, and the 'terror' which they and their accompanying revolutionary courts subsequently imposed.

That students should have been so passionately engaged with a Revolution that many came to see as regressive also sheds light on some of the contradictions of the revolutionary movement which Tocqueville, two centuries earlier, had so astutely observed. The Shah had launched his 'White Revolution' with a view to managing a social and economic transformation of the country that would in turn catalyse a political change, one that would inexorably follow and by all accounts be bloodless. He had initially warned against starting a 'revolution' but then embraced the project with all the zeal of the convert. He had proceeded, however, with little enthusiasm for political reform, at least the sort that democratic theorists would endorse, preferring instead to consolidate his own authority as the spiritual head of his nation, and the emphasis on the first-person singular was noticeably increasing (the Shah, for example, would frequently talk of 'my' oil).

The White Revolution, aided by the massive increase in oil revenues, had delivered a socio-economic transformation of the country – not always as the planners had foreseen, but a transformation, nonetheless. Urbanization and industrialization had accelerated, and education had boomed with the foundation of new universities, but also a huge expansion in the number of students – on government grants – abroad. By the end of the 1970s, there were an estimated 50,000 students studying in the United States, with upwards of 25,000 in universities in Europe. The

Shah had severely constrained the available political space in Iran and young people were not encouraged to go into politics, or indeed to study subjects that might encourage them to do so. The Shah wanted technocrats, not bureaucrats of the old school, and was keen on boosting scientific proficiency. The irony of this was that the clarity provided by a scientific education, unlike the pervasive ambiguity and nuance of an education in the humanities, encouraged many students to adhere to the radical (scientific) clarity provided by Marxism and Islamism – or, indeed, a mixture of the two. There was in their minds a right or wrong answer, and increasingly the Shah was the wrong answer.

The structure of the reforms the Shah had implemented was therefore not to his long-term advantage, and even the basis of the White Revolution – land reform – had resulted in reforms that might centralize his power but would ultimately weaken his authority, as frustrated rural workers either drifted into shanty towns or engaged wearily with the faceless Ministry for Agriculture. For all his impatience to reach his Great Civilization, however, the Shah was not unaware of the need to engage in a measure of genuine political reform, not least because, much like his own father, he had little confidence that his own son would be able to govern as he had done, even if such a development was desirable. Indeed, there were many within the Court who felt that, while this particular leopard would never change his spots, there was a real possibility of reform with the accession of the new king, and certainly the Empress Farah (the Shah's third wife, whom he married in 1959) was regarded as a more liberal, progressive individual.

There has been a view that, much as with President Kennedy, the arrival of the new Democratic President Carter encouraged the Shah to consider liberalizing the political process, but there were indications that he had already been thinking about this before Carter's election and that, somewhat counter-intuitively, his establishment of the 'Rastakhiz' party was an indication of a new direction of travel. But this attempt to control political reform was precisely the problem with his entire strategy, which few outside his inner circle really believed in. That said, from 1977 there was a belief, including in the diplomatic community, that the Shah had decided on a policy of gradual reform with some limited opening up of political space to allow for some measured criticism of the government – if not the Shah. Political rivalries within the State encouraged this opening of debate, especially as the economy began, as predicted, to overheat and falter. The response was not quite what the Shah, notoriously thin skinned, had expected. Rather than criticizing the government and expressing their love for the 'father of the nation', student organizations and intellectuals began openly to voice criticisms of the system itself.

The Shah was nonplussed by developments – having convinced himself that his people loved him, he was not quite sure how best to react but, rather than tighten the screws again, decided that the only course was to press on. The process of liberalization was never going to be a tidy affair, and at the end of the day the Shah felt sufficiently secure to continue, certain in his own mind of the path he had chosen. If some might have reservations, few if any would express them. At New Year 1977, validation came in the form of a flying visit from President Carter, who, in what was regarded as something of a diplomatic coup, had decided there was no better friend to spend New Year's Eve with than the Shah. The festivities were to become infamous, given what followed. Carter, acutely aware that the Shah had been uncertain of his support, decided to compensate by offering fulsome praise for the Shah and his regime, describing Iran as an 'island of stability' in an otherwise troubled region. As the standard narrative of the Revolution goes, this endorsement encouraged the Shah to take aim at his most vocal critic: Ayatollah Khomeini.

Hindsight tells us that Khomeini was the leader of the revolution that toppled the Shah a year later, but at the turn of 1978, Khomeini, while far from unknown, was but one of a variety of opponents who lay just over the horizon. He held a special status, given his clerical background, but even those who gravitated around him regarded him as a means to an end – a symbol, rather than an active leader. His dedicated followers, needless to say, saw things differently and the Shah's irritation with him ensured that Khomeini's status could only be enhanced. On 8 January 1978, a date which the textbooks tell us witnessed the start of the Islamic Revolution – not that anyone noticed at the time – an anonymous article was placed in the newspaper *Etelaat*, which accused Khomeini of a variety of sins, including that of being a traitor and not a real Iranian. The insults elicited a strong reaction in the seminary city of Qom where Khomeini had lived and taught before he went into exile, with protests against the Shah. What became immediately apparent was not the strength of the protests, but how unprepared the State was to deal with them. If the Shah proudly boasted of having the fifth-largest armed forces in the world, with one of the most advanced air forces, these were not much good at policing and crowd control. With casualties resulting from the use of live fire, a pattern emerged in which subsequent protests would be organized on the fortieth day after the death of the initial victim.

Be that as it may, until high summer few people thought they were facing a serious political upheaval, let alone a revolution. Government continued and, in a sign of confidence, the British ambassador departed on a three-month vacation, not returning until September, when he discovered the political situation had taken a dramatic turn for the worse. The Shah, who had made himself the lynchpin of the system, without whom no decision could be made, was found to be dangerously indecisive, often giving contradictory signals to his security forces and the public at

large. All this made him a mockery to the revolutionaries and contrasted sharply with the clarity provided
by Khomeini, who simply reiterated his demand for
a return to the 'constitution'. Which 'constitution'
was conveniently left unsaid, and, in many ways,
Khomeini deployed an ambiguity cloaked in clarity,
since those who knew him realized he was not talking
of the Constitution of 1906. The Shah's continued
prevarications, however, were a gift to Khomeini, who
continued to define his own principled stance with
the Shah's own apparent moral ambiguity.

One particularly egregious event occurred in August
when the Cinema Rex in Abadan was set on fire,
resulting in the death of some 400 people. Everyone
assumed that the State security services had been
behind the attack. The Shah, horrified at what had
happened, immediately dismissed the government
and brought in an emollient elder statesman with
assurances of reform. The reality, it soon transpired,
was that the fire had been started by religious zealots,
but by the time this emerged matters had moved on.
The new government of Sharif-Emami attempted to
dampen the religious enthusiasm of the movement
by closing down casinos; restricting publications
considered offensive to Muslim sensibilities, while
freeing up the press in general; and legalizing political
parties, to engage in political debate. Most dramatically, the imperial calendar introduced with much
pomp in 1976 was now unceremoniously dumped.
All this, of course, empowered the revolutionaries,

while causing increasing anxiety among supporters who recalled that, in a previous crisis, the Shah had swiftly departed for a holiday abroad.

The Shah, meanwhile, had been persuaded to show a bit of backbone and decided to impose martial law, but this resulted in an even worse calamity when protesters were shot while demonstrating in Jaleh Square in Tehran. The Jaleh Square massacre, as it became known, deeply affected the Shah, whose morale, already badly dented, was now blown. The government attested that some eighty-six people had been killed – a figure that approximated to the later confirmed number of eighty-eight – while the opposition claimed the figure was in the thousands. Irrespective of the numbers, the Shah was distraught at the blood that had been spilt and effectively lost his nerve. The opposition, sensing weakness, moved in for the kill. The Shah's supporters began to make arrangements to move abroad, while those who had remained studiously neutral in the struggle decided that discretion was no longer the better part of valour and joined the protests. Saddam Hussein, meanwhile, offered to dispose of Khomeini for the Shah, who politely demurred and asked instead that the recalcitrant cleric be expelled. Not sure where to go, Khomeini ended up in Paris where, despite French insistence that he refrain from political activity, his supporters established a base with full access to the international media.

Indeed, from late October, it was clear to most observers that Iran was in the throes of a revolutionary upheaval that had seemingly crept up on them from nowhere. The Shah was good enough to confirm this by making a formal address in which he notified his people that he had 'heard the sound of their revolution' and that he would stand by them. If anything signalled imminent demise, this was it. As if to confirm this prognosis, the government, in a bid to placate the opposition, began arresting loyal officials – including the then Minister of Court and former Prime Minister Amir Abbas Hoveida – and releasing its opponents. In the words of one minister at the time, it was a most 'perverse' situation. Foreign governments, not least that of the United States, took heed and began to make preparations for a transition, even if the speed of collapse was taking everyone by surprise. Hopes abounded that a peaceful transition may still prevail and, while hopes of a regency under the Empress seemed wildly misplaced, some felt that a transition to a democratic republic was a possibility. Khomeini, for his part, emphasized that a government guided by Islam would be a constitutional one.

On 16 January 1979, barely a year after the misjudged article, the Shah departed on a one-way holiday into exile. The caretaker government he had left in place to manage things barely lasted out the month as the army declared its neutrality and Khomeini returned to ecstatic crowds two weeks later on 1 February, establishing his own provisional government. The Shah had gone, in a dramatic unwinding of authority that had left many bewildered – not least because, so far, it had been comparatively bloodless. Despite the wilder claims of the revolutionaries, later assessments showed that, from 1963 to the departure of the Shah, a total of 3,164 had died in all forms of resistance. Of those, 2,781 had died in the disturbances throughout 1978, with all but 731 of these being in Tehran.[2] The Revolution had triumphed, but it was far from over. The bloodletting was about to begin.

Like revolutions before it, what became known as the 'Islamic Revolution' now entered a phase of definition, where the competing wings of the movement that had been united in their desire to rid themselves of the Shah now fought each other for dominance, not only politically but ideologically. Most people knew what they did not want, but few knew what they wanted, and when people voted in a referendum to abolish the monarchy and establish an 'Islamic Republic', few had any idea what that meant in practice. Some argued that it was a mere semantic distinction, providing the new republic with a degree of Iranian authenticity that suggested no more than Montesquieu's virtuous republic. Others, including Khomeini, had more concrete ideas about clerical control of the State, and if some people failed to take the idea of the Guardianship of the Jurist (*velayat-e faqih*) seriously, Khomeini was not one of them.

The first few months of the Revolution, known as the spring of freedom, saw many of these ideas thrashed out in public, while the more committed revolutionaries took revenge on the *ancien régime*. The revolutionaries were surprised to find a number of senior officials languishing in prison following their incarceration in the last months of the Shah's rule, a breathtaking act of neglect on the Shah's part. These officials, including the hapless Hoveida and several senior military and security personnel, were subjected to sham trials and swiftly executed. The provisional government protested. Khomeini dismissed these as misplaced, in a clear sign that ideals and reality were about to diverge widely. Indeed, Khomeini's own protestations that, as a humble teacher, he would soon retire to continue his profession in Qom – a claim that appeared to earn him the moniker of the 'Gandhi of Iran' from a number of US officials – soon seemed disingenuous, as neither he nor his supporters were keen on his retirement anywhere. The scale of the crowds that had greeted him on his return had certainly had an effect, and Khomeini was clear that it was his vision that would triumph.

Initial drafts of the new constitution, based on that of the French Fifth Republic, had not included Khomeini's own trademark idea for governance, and over the year he battled to get this in. By the end of that year, the draft had been revisited to present the public with a constitution that married the best of the West with the indigenous, Islamic qualities that made the constitution distinctive. It would be a unique synergy between 'Islamic' and 'republican' values and institutions, bringing back religion for what Iran's new revolutionary ideologues considered to be the postmodern age. They were certainly not short of aspiration or ambition, declaring their revolution to be the third great revolution after that of France and of Russia, with others claiming that the now Islamic Revolution marked the greatest leap forward in human thought since the Renaissance. Few noticed at the time how stubbornly embedded these narratives were within a European historical framework, a clear indication that the Revolution was not quite as transformative as some pretended. Nonetheless, if those who supported the republican interpretation of the Revolution sought to make this marriage of ideas work, the Islamists saw it as little more than a union of temporary inconvenience.

To ensure the frictions could be overcome, however, the authorities resorted to a tried and tested method: a foreign entanglement. The Revolution had drawn on three principal trends, none of which could be cleanly distinguished, but which can be broadly defined as Marxist, Islamist and secular nationalist. The latter were soon squeezed out of the race for dominance, being both liberal in outlook and small in number, leaving the Red and Black (to quote the Shah) to fight it out. This soon took on the character of a fully fledged civil conflict with thousands of deaths, made all the more vicious by the claim that the internecine fighting was undermining Revolution at a time of foreign threat. The first rendition of this foreign threat was self-inflicted; the other, mismanaged. Both were to have a profound impact on the development of the Revolution.

The considerable contribution of the Left to the Revolution gave the movement a strongly anti-imperialist tone and in the first few weeks a number of Western embassies, including that of the United States, came under attack, only for Khomeini to urge the zealous students to vacate the premises. By November, however, with tensions rising over the future direction of travel, an opportunity presented itself when Carter decided, against his own political judgement, to allow the cancer-ridden Shah into the United States for treatment. Iran's revolutionaries, in the excessively febrile politics of the moment, concluded that the United States was conspiring to return the Shah in the manner of 1953, and 'Students in the Line of the Imam' decided to stage a protest by launching yet another assault on the US Embassy.

It is a remarkable fact that even at this stage the United States was trying to manage the transition. The embassy of old had been reduced substantially in size, with a new core of staff with particular expertise in Iran, many of whom had volunteered to be a witness to history. Right up until October 1979, the provisional government was receiving intelligence briefings from US officials, some of which pointed to Iraqi military movements near the Iranian border.[3] Much of this was, of course, dismissed by Iranian officials as scaremongering but, be that as it may, it seemed that if the US stayed the course, they might weather the storm. It was to prove an extraordinarily optimistic ambition. On 4 November, students scaled the Embassy walls, meeting a somewhat passive response until it became apparent that they were carrying guns. The American chargé d'affaires, Bruce Laingen, was at that very moment in the Iranian Foreign Ministry and, notified of the events, requested that the government take action to evict them.

On this occasion, however, the government found itself outmanoeuvred by Khomeini, who surprised everyone by declaring his support for the students. The provisional government felt it had no choice but to resign. The students, who subsequently claimed that they had not anticipated staying for more than a few days, found themselves at the centre of an international storm that was to last 444 days. For Khomeini, this foreign entanglement did the trick, diverting attention and also allowing the regime to clamp down on dissent. Above all, it showed where real power lay in the new Islamic Republic. Caught off guard, the Americans had frantically shredded any sensitive documents, but had no time to burn them. To add insult to injury, the students patiently sifted through the material, pasted it back together again and published it. The humiliation broadcast nightly into American homes was complete, with Khomeini only authorizing the release some 15 minutes after Carter's nemesis in the election in 1980, Ronald Reagan, was sworn into office in January 1981.

War

Some have conjectured that the timing was deliberately intended to hurt Carter, and it undoubtedly left deep scars on the Democratic Party. But another view is that, not for the last time, the Iranians vastly overplayed their hand. In September 1980, Saddam Hussein, itching to take revenge for what he considered to be the imposition of the 1975 Algiers Agreement regarding the sovereignty of the Shatt al-Arab waterway, decided now would be an opportune time to change the geopolitical relationship. Faced with provocations from the revolutionary government, which was repeatedly urging Iraq's Shia to rise up against the tyrant, Saddam felt he had an adequate *casus belli* and, on 1 September, he invaded the oil-rich province of Khuzestan, in the hope and expectation that Iranian Arabs would rise up in support. Saddam Hussein had tried to frame this as a liberation by inducing a number of Arab Iranians to engage in what was to prove a fatal seizure of the Iranian Embassy in London earlier that summer. As with that exercise, the invasion was to prove another fatal miscalculation.

Iranians were somewhat taken aback by Saddam Hussein's impertinence, and few believed that Iraq would dare to attack Iran without some wider international instigation. On one level of course they were correct, although they singularly failed to see their own role in facilitating this. Their continued occupation of the US Embassy, in complete contravention of all diplomatic norms, meant that Iran had few friends in diplomatic circles, and when the UN Security Council was approached to condemn the invasion, it demurred, confirming to Iranians that a conspiracy was afoot. Saddam Hussein was not condemned, but the Iranians were themselves complicit in this sin of omission. Khomeini was quick to see the onset of war as a 'blessing', a comment that has since raised a few eyebrows. But, from a political point of view, it was just the sort of foreign distraction that could unify the country in a common cause. The Shah had gone, and in his place came a tyrant all Iranians, even those who disliked the Revolution, could oppose. It was not to be the last time the regime turned to nationalism to consolidate its position.

Its initial problem was reconstituting the armed forces, depleted through purges and desertion. The revolutionary government had found a reason to be cheerful for the enormous weapons purchases made by the Shah, and it also had to hand the new Islamic Revolutionary Guards Corps (IRGC), an ad hoc religiously egalitarian unit of revolutionary zealots with minimal organization but ideological determination. They were the ideal unit to send down to defend the cities of Khuzestan in the brutal urban warfare that was developing. In the midst of this crisis, the US hostages found themselves to be surplus to requirements – and a diplomatic handicap, to boot – so a resolution had to be found.

Saddam Hussein soon discovered that his triumphant march had stalled, and over the next two years the IRGC and a rehabilitated army fought ruthlessly to evict the Iraqis from Iranian territory. By 1982, the Iranians proudly proclaimed the liberation of Khorramshahr. It was an empowering moment – the first time in modern history that the Iranians had shown themselves competent in war. Now, some argued, was the time to terminate hostilities and refocus energies on rebuilding the country. More zealous voices, however, prevailed, and Khomeini, declaring that the road to Jerusalem lay through Karbala, authorized the continuation of the war with an offensive into Iraq. War aims were now defined as the overthrow of Saddam Hussein, making it an existential struggle for the dictator, who swiftly turned it into an Arab–Persian war, calling on all Arabs to come to his aid. Only Syria declined.

The decision to continue the war has become one of the most controversial in contemporary Iran, in many ways second only to the decision to accept the UN-brokered ceasefire some six years later. One's politics has tended to define one's position on these two issues, with the hawks arguing that the war should have been continued to victory, and that the agreement to cease hostilities was a great betrayal imposed by greedy politicians on a military that still had much fight left in it. The reality was much more sanguine, as the military leaders of those times reiterate on a regular basis. Iran was bled dry in six years of brutal warfare, and while the level of casualties has been exaggerated for political effect, the truth of the matter was that Iran had neither material nor political stamina left to continue, and many among the leadership worried that the revolutionary project itself might be undermined.

The consequences of the war on the economy and wider society were profound. Leaving aside the opportunity costs of a war that would not have been fought had the Revolution not happened, and that was in the event fought with few if any allies, the eight-year Iran–Iraq War was the first near-total war the Iranians had been engaged in. Society was mobilized and civilians were targeted in a war that saw missiles rain down on Iranian cities and the threat of a chemical weapons attack taken seriously. In addition to the regular armed forces, which were now rehabilitated and provided much of the planning and logistical work of the war, the IRGC expanded exponentially, to parallel the army with a view to reaping the spoils after the war was over. Much to the army's irritation, the authorities frequently credited the IRGC with successful operations they were at best partners in. To these were added the Basij militia, which drew on those deemed unsuitable for the main military units, young and old, and which presented the world with the sans-culottes of revolutionary Iran. In terms of the sheer weight of casualties, it was the Basij that often took the brunt, engaging in human-wave attacks that drew comparisons with the Great War, though

Soviet tactics in the Second World War might have been a better parallel.

In terms of the fighting at the front, and the static lines that soon emerged, the Great War analogies seemed apposite, especially when it became apparent that the Iraqis were using chemical weapons. The brutality of the fighting was comparable, even if the extent of casualties was not. The government's own statistics, rarely broadcast, indicated the total number of fatalities over the eight-year conflict lay somewhere between 188,000 and 220,000, considerably less than the number of British deaths (c.800,000) over the four years of the Great War.[4] These were unprecedented figures for Iran and take little account of the wounded (living martyrs, as they were called) or the psychological trauma of the war on the combatants. But the determination to exaggerate even these tragic figures had a clear political purpose of emphasizing the popular sacrifice, with the aim of legitimizing the Revolution. Henceforth, policies could be promoted or condemned with the refrain that they respected or insulted the blood of the martyrs. The chief beneficiary of all this was of course the IRGC, for the Iran–Iraq War was to become a foundation myth they would exploit relentlessly.

But the other more interesting consequence of the war, which was a matter of some consternation for the authorities, was the social impact. The authorities used the war as a means of suppressing dissent and imposing a measure of Islamic austerity

– the mandatory veiling of women, for example, was imposed in 1983 – but as the war progressed and fatigue began to set in, the government was forced to adjust its policies and to respond more clearly and emphatically to nationalist sentiment. Much as in the Soviet Union in 1941, the war against Iraq became increasingly a matter of patriotism. At the same time as more men were sent to the front, so women began to fill the vacated jobs, giving them a more prominent role than more hard-line Islamists would have liked. But perhaps most troubling for the more astute among the leadership was the change the war was making to general mentalities. Deference was becoming a thing of the past as many veterans returned from the front demanding something better from their government. But, more than that, the educational policies of the previous fifty years were bearing fruit. Iranians were more literate and, through new technologies, more connected. They were less acquiescent subjects and becoming more questioning citizens.

When Ayatollah Khomeini took the fateful decision to end the war, it was a decision that lacked the controversy it would acquire in later years. Economic and political pressures were mounting. The US was increasingly intervening in the Persian Gulf and the accidental shooting down of Iran Air 655 with all 290 passengers caused widespread shock. The country was exhausted, and the general feeling was that to continue would only bring the legitimacy of the regime into question. People were already asking why it had been continued for so long, and Khomeini felt it prudent to state that, while 'the war had fault, no one was responsible', to avoid recriminations. For all the economic damage, Iran, having been subject to sanctions (as a result of the hostage crisis), found itself in much better economic shape than its rival, without extensive overseas debts. Above all, the country had survived. But this resulted in some misplaced self-congratulation, insofar as the leadership regarded this as a testament to the country's revolutionary spirit rather than to the fact that they had inherited a robust State system from the Pahlavis. The misreading of this political reality would, in time, cost them dearly.

6

Building an Islamic Republic (1989–2000)

The war, naturally, relegated many of the important political debates about the future direction of the country to the margins. The marriage of inconvenience between Islam and the Republic, the fundamental friction at the heart of the constitution, functioned under the watchful eye of Ayatollah Khomeini's leadership, and his charisma effectively subsumed and disguised any problems that might arise. The presidency was largely ceremonial at this stage, since much of the arbitration needed to make the system work was devolved on Khomeini as 'Supreme Leader'. Although the 'Guardianship' was meant to operate as some sort of ethical supervisor, Khomeini's peculiar position as the founder of the Revolution meant that he could basically define the role as he wished, and his inclination, as well as that of his supporters, was to be more hands-on.

As with the Shah, his supporters claimed he had no choice, because 'people' were simply unwilling to take responsibility. But, like the Shah, this was a partial explanation. Both were instinctive autocrats with a determination to shape the country in their own image, but their means of operation were different. While the Shah was impatient with committees,

Khomeini positively encouraged them, although not as a means to encourage corporate governance, but as a means of allowing him to arbitrate. The results were very much the same, even if the process was more Byzantine. Ultimately, people appealed to Khomeini for a decision – he always insisted on the last word – and soon learnt how to appeal to his sensibilities. Khomeini was better at reaching decisions, but often couched his answers in ambiguities that his acolytes would then compete to interpret according to what they felt were his wishes. This made for poor government, but allowed Khomeini plausible deniability if the outcomes were not politically satisfactory. This process could be seen in his late endorsement of the seizure of the US Embassy, and led to oddities such as newspapers being closed down because he had complained about a particular article.

Before his death in 1989, which led to widespread bewilderment and genuine grief, Khomeini bequeathed three distinct legacies to his successors. All have proved enormously controversial, and, needless to say, are open to interpretation. The first reflected his response to the continued frictions between the organs of government, with the declaration that in any conflict the interests of the Islamic government must come first, noting that this applied even if it meant that various Muslim obligations – such as pilgrimage – had to be suspended. This was read at the time as a vindication of 'secular' government but, as time would reveal, it all depended on whose hands government lay in. One immediate consequence was the formation of yet another 'committee', the Expediency Council, a body of the great and the good whose job was to arbitrate disputes. Since the last word remained with the Supreme Leader, this authority to arbitrate was essentially advisory. The consequences of this decision were, like many things in the Islamic Republic, slow to reveal themselves.

The second legacy – the fatwa against Salman Rushdie – had a far more immediate impact and was controversial from the start, with even the current President and future Supreme Leader, Ali Khamenei, suggesting that if Rushdie apologized all might be forgiven. He was swiftly rebuked by Khomeini. The decision to murder a writer for a book he had written, for all its international repercussions, paled into insignificance when compared to a much darker, if hidden, moment in the young Republic's history: the summary execution of around 4,000 political prisoners as a means of 'tidying' things up before the war ended and normality returned.

The ostensible justification for this exercise in mass murder was an ill-judged 'invasion' by members of the Islamic Marxist group, the Mojahedin-e Khalq, who, after the violent civil unrest in the aftermath of the Revolution, had unwisely relocated to Iraq. The attack was swiftly defeated, and Khomeini took the opportunity to visit punishment on its members languishing in prison, as well as many other members of the Left, convening a four-man 'death committee', including an ambitious young Judiciary official, Ebrahim Raisi, to oversee the process.

The 'process' was, of course, little more than a farce, but the outrage would not have seen the light of day had Khomeini's heir apparent, Ayatollah Montazeri, not protested against the executions as an abomination that would come to haunt the Islamic Republic. This and his intervention in the Iran–Contra affair, the exposure of which severely embarrassed Reagan and the Republican Party, resulted in Montazeri's removal from the succession. In later years, more details would emerge from Montazeri's office, including a recording of him berating members of the 'committee'. He would be replaced by the then President, swiftly elevated to the rank of 'Ayatollah', Ali Khamenei.

Rafsanjani

Khamenei's surprising succession was regarded at the time as a political sleight of hand by the nimble Ali Akbar Hashemi Rafsanjani, a mid-level cleric, known for his pragmatism and private wealth. Following Khomeini's death, it was Rafsanjani who effectively institutionalized the Islamic Republic, attempting to secure its foundations while pursuing policies that were pregnant with difficulties for the future. Several important changes were made to the constitution, the first being the removal of the post of Prime Minister, ensuring that the presidency henceforth would enjoy executive power. In addition, the qualification 'absolute' was prefixed to the position of the Guardianship, with the intention of shoring up Khamenei's authority vis-à-vis more senior and reactionary clerics who might object to other religious reforms. (Rafsanjani would later, and fatefully, also oversee the empowerment of the oversight body known as the Guardian Council, whose role was to vet laws for religious compatibility, with extra powers to vet candidates for election in the belief that this would ensure more extreme characters could be prevented from running. In the event, it did the opposite.) Rafsanjani saw himself as the younger Khamenei's mentor, who would as a result be guided down a more progressive path. This 'second republic', as some authors have described it, seemed primed for an economic renaissance after the war. With a merchant-cleric in charge, the Islamic Revolution was about to enter its Thermidorean phase.

The problems of the Islamic Republic have often been over-complicated, partly as a result of the realities of its government, but also as a reflection of the need of some analysts to engage in Kremlinology, to indulge the incoherence of government in Iran by attempting to turn a vice into a virtue. The complexities of government are, as a result, often ascribed to a democratic turn. This is not the case. They reflect a continued inability or unwillingness to take responsibilities for decisions, with a view to passing matters up the chain of command. Ultimately, the only person able to handle this Gordian Knot is the Supreme Leader, and the more supreme the Leader becomes, the easier this becomes. The system is a recipe for autocracy. In the 1990s, however, the Supreme Leader was still finding his feet and Rafsanjani had some room for manoeuvre. His chief problems, which have remained largely consistent, were dealing with the legacy of the war and the purpose of the Revolution. Was it to provide an Islamic *Republic* or an Islamic *State*? And, given that decision, what was the best way to achieve it?

These fundamental questions have been at the heart of the political frictions that have effectively brought Iran to its knees over the last few decades. Rafsanjani and his successor as President, Mohammad Khatami, were firm believers in the Islamic *Republic*, and argued vigorously for a strengthening of those republican institutions with a concomitant weakening and eventual removal of revolutionary organizations that should have become redundant. The argument with which many in the political and intellectual elite of the Islamic Republic were engaged throughout the 1990s focused on the nature of Islam, and how religion might best be integrated into the republican structures of the State. The conclusion reached would have been familiar to many in the West who over the centuries had grappled with similar ideas.

The marriage between Islam and the Republic had been justified on the grounds that politics had to have an ethical oversight, but others were concluding that the effect was to politicize religion, and consequently weaken it in the eyes of the people. If Islam was seen to be at the core of the State's activities, if the State got things wrong then the people would naturally conclude that Islam was to blame. In order to shield Islam and protect the purity of religion, it would be better to distinguish them. This appeared remarkably similar to those arguments for secularism and the separation of Church and State. In this reading, the Islamic character of the State would be shaped by the fact that its principal functionaries were Muslims and their faith informed their actions. It was not necessary to have religious institutions, which on the contrary would in the long run serve to undermine the faith, on the principle that power corrupts.

Unsurprisingly, this line of thinking would ultimately lead to a marginalization and probable removal of the Guardianship of the Jurist, and there were voices raised about the uniqueness of the position for Khomeini, and the suggestion that after Khamenei the position would become redundant. This was, of course, anathema to those who felt the entire purpose of the Revolution was the establishment of an Islamic State around the figure of the Supreme Jurist, who they stressed was 'absolute' not for the specific purposes of contending with more reactionary clerics (as Rafsanjani had imagined), but in uninhibited constitutional terms. This debate was to continue with increasing vigour throughout the 1990s, and to come to a head during the presidency of the reformist Mohammad Khatami (1997–2005), but for the duration of Rafsanjani's presidency (1989–97), Khamenei and his supporters were too weak to pose a serious challenge, while Rafsanjani remained popular among the elites and moved with a degree of caution.

Rafsanjani's approach to development was remarkably similar to that of the Shah he had done so much to overthrow. Eschewing the dangers of politics, he had decided on economic development to catalyse change, digging out and implementing plans that had first been conceived in the 1970s. The then mayor of Tehran, Gholamhossein Karbaschi, acknowledged this by crediting his Pahlavi predecessor, Gholamreza Nikpay, for the urban reconstruction of the city he was pursuing, omitting to mention that Nikpay had been summarily executed in the Revolution.

Rafsanjani even tried to find commercial bridges to the United States. Unfortunately for Rafsanjani, the Clinton administration, with its institutional memory of the hostage crisis, found any engagement with Iran to be politically toxic, and when the US oil company Conoco was invited to sign an oil contract with Iran, it was swiftly ostracized, with sanctions on commercial ties rapidly passed by the US Congress. Rebuffed, Rafsanjani turned to Europe, though even here relations were to prove to be complicated by both the ongoing Rushdie fatwa, and the fact that Iranian intelligence agents were busy settling scores with Iranian dissidents on European soil. In many ways, it was remarkable that these events did not completely rule out commercial relations with Iran, but it is also a reminder that, at this stage, for all the

US animosity, the Europeans remained wedded to the idea of engagement.

The activities of Iranian operatives abroad reflected a broader problem with governance in the aftermath of the Iran–Iraq War. Quite apart from the persistence of a war mentality which left many unable to adjust to the realities of peacetime, there was a sense, especially among the revolutionary hardliners, that the 'struggle' continued, albeit in different forms. It was clear that Rafsanjani found it difficult to contain some of these elements and, in an attempt at reform which he would come to rue, he decided that one way to contain the fall-out would be to merge the IRGC into the regular armed forces, forcing it to effectively conform to a hierarchy, structure and discipline. This attempt collided with another innovative means of squaring the economic circle.

Although the opportunity costs of the Iran–Iraq War were enormous (estimates vary), the Islamic Republic had emerged from the war in much better economic shape than its rival. But be that as it may, the coffers were found to be wanting. Rafsanjani's solution to this was to encourage various institutions, including the security establishment, to supplement their income through fines and economic ventures. This, ironically, strengthened the hand of the IRGC and its associated organizations vis-à-vis the regular armed forces, since they were better networked and socially connected. The informality of the IRGC worked to its benefit. The consequence was that, over time, the IRGC subsumed the regular armed forces, rather than the other way round, exemplifying a process which over time saw republican institutions weakened in the face of revolutionary aggrandizement.

This also reflected two other tendencies which grew to dominate. First, there was a political reaction from those revolutionary institutions unwilling to be sidelined. Just as hardliners gathered around the person of Khamenei, so too did they find common cause with the more revolutionary elements in the IRGC. But the real problem was money and its distribution. The new State had acquired considerable assets from the departing imperial family, as well as properties from those who had fled the country after 1979 or had simply had their assets seized. These assets were now run by religious foundations accountable to Khamenei alone. Paying no tax, and with political and by extension economic access, they effectively had licences to print money. Rafsanjani wanted to curtail their activities, or at least make them more transparent. Naturally, they were resistant to this idea, and they enjoyed an advantage in that Rafsanjani's own economic activities were less than transparent. He had come to prominence as a thoroughly commercial cleric with a finger in many pies, for whom making money was a positive attribute. This proved attractive for many after the austerity of revolution and war, but it proved an albatross around his neck. Unwilling to lead by example, he compromised on this important principle to the detriment of all. The result was that the revolutionary institutions, far from being brought under institutional control, grew richer and more powerful, providing the glue for an agglomeration of hardliners around the person of the Supreme Leader.

Reform

Rafsanjani, regarded as a traditional conservative, took much of the blame for what was seen as a return to imperial decadence. His propensity to reintroduce ceremony was regarded as a dangerous betrayal of revolutionary principles and he was popularly derided as 'Akbar Shah'. But, fatally for him, his attempt to bring the revolutionary institutions under control while at the same time refusing to become transparent about his own wealth ensured that he would increasingly come under attack from both left and right.

For the Left, the charges were again familiar. His attempts to pursue economic reform in the absence of a political framework were doomed to fail and, much as in the 1970s, what would result was corruption. Unlike in the 1970s, however, financial corruption soon became a *sine qua non* of the revolutionary Right, whose distaste for transparency and accountability was held up as a virtue of informality and revolutionary integrity. To say it was perverse would be an understatement. But Rafsanjani had one last throw of the dice.

Unable to run for a third term, he threw his weight behind his former Minister of Culture, the unassuming Mohammad Khatami, whose love of books and learning (he had also been head of the National Library) had earned him the contempt of his opponents. A cleric from the Left, Khatami had studied Western philosophy and, like his mentor, was a strong supporter of the principles of the Republic, while recognizing that political and economic reforms had to go hand in hand.

Regarded very much as an outlier in 1997, with support from Rafsanjani, Khatami surprised the establishment in storming to an electoral victory in what amounted to the fairest election to have been held in the Islamic Republic of Iran to date. Khatami had in fact persuaded his critics to allow him to run on the basis that he could maximize the turnout and thus reinforce the popular legitimacy of the Islamic Republic – elections until then having been relatively lacklustre and controlled events. In the event, his shock landslide victory exceeded expectations and concurrently maximized fear among those who viewed the 'Republic' with trepidation.

The excitement caused by Khatami's victory was palpable among a populace seeking normalcy. It was as if a new dawn had arrived. For hardliners, it was the worst possible result insofar as it confirmed that the population were not the revolutionary Islamists they believed them to be. The first of Khatami's two terms witnessed the most dramatic liberalization of Iranian society since the turbulent days of oil nationalization under Dr Mosaddeq.

Drawing their inspiration from the Constitutional Revolution of 1906, reformists boasted that they were finally delivering on that promise: a constitutional system which reconciled tradition with modernity, cognizant of the realities of the Iranian inheritance while open to the opportunities of the future. The press multiplied on a scale hitherto unknown, and literary magazines and journals proliferated. Ideas, the lifeblood of a dynamic society, flourished, with intellectuals free to discuss the nature of religion and its wider relationship to society, the merits of secularism and, more provocatively, the question of toleration and the validity of the death penalty in Islamic Law. Most egregious for the most devout among the establishment was the argument against the continuing relevance of apostasy, seen as a red line for many senior clerics, as well as the view that unquestioning 'emulation' – the process by which the faithful would follow the dictates of a particular senior cleric – was out of tune with a progressive, intellectually liberating age. For some, and for a limited time at least, it appeared that nothing was off limits.

Strikingly, when it became apparent that rogue elements in the Intelligence Ministry had been murdering dissident intellectuals, Khatami ordered an investigation and subsequently purged the Ministry of its undesirable elements. Many of these elements were to simply move across to other more hard-line institutions, such as the Judiciary and IRGC, where they helped establish rival security agencies, but – for the time being at least – it appeared as if the President was taking decisive action to eradicate those rotten apples in the body politic of the Republic.

Iran's image abroad was also being remade. Khatami was a cleric and an avowed supporter of 'Islamic Democracy', but international viewers were surprised to discover that his understanding of that concept was firmly within an Anglo-American model of secularism, famously quoting Alexis de Tocqueville's *Democracy in America* during an interview on CNN in 1998. If Iranian hardliners found all this suspect, Westerners were bewildered by it all – not least the Americans, who found this new outreach incomprehensible. French observers likewise were at once impressed and confused by his admiration for the Enlightenment.

Much of this was symbolic, of course, but in one international engagement Khatami scored a notable if unheralded success, and that was the resolution of the Rushdie fatwa with the United Kingdom. In this case, the Iranian government agreed not to pursue its implementation on the basis that religious injunctions bore no relation to the government. Although not commented on at the time, the Iranian government had effectively, through a diplomatic sleight of hand, acknowledged the separation of religion and politics.

For all his bonhomie, however, Khatami soon realized that, equally, political reform without economic change was just as fruitless as Rafsanjani's approach. There was no point preaching transparency and accountability in politics if vast wealth was kept beyond the scrutiny of government bodies, and many wondered why these religious foundations remained untaxed when the government was struggling to make ends meet. These foundations were accountable to the Supreme Leader alone, were often afforded preferential exchange rates for imports and were fast becoming corrupt business conglomerates. The Foundation of the Oppressed, for example, was widely mocked for importing luxury cars.

While hardliners found all this discomforting and at odds with their own vision of the Revolution, they did not initially find it an immediate threat to their own interests. As long as Khatami improved Iran's image and talked a good talk, with the occasional walk, they could see the merit in his presidency. Their strategy was one of containment and obstructionism. But his move to purge the Intelligence Ministry and his growing criticism of the economic malaise (corruption) that underpinned the State – not least those unaccountable revolutionary organs of the State – was beginning to elicit a more serious reaction. Reformism was increasingly being defined as a heresy that needed to be uprooted, and the belief in the utility of the 'Republic' for hardliners began to wane rapidly. For Khatami and his allies, on the other hand, it was clear that the root of the problem lay here, and that a wholesale restricting of the political economy was necessary. Talk began to circulate about further 'necessary' amendment to the constitution to eradicate incongruities that were inhibiting the government's ability to act.

By the end of the 1990s, Iran was back exporting oil, but the lack of investment and a low oil price meant that government revenue was constrained. The fundamental problem was the structure of the Iranian economy, which was built on trade rather than investment. The former relied on a degree of volatility and opaqueness to maximize profits, while the latter required stability and transparency. For people to invest, not least foreigners, one had to grant access to accounts, but since many revolutionary institutions and foundations were reluctant to let their own government review the books, there was no chance of a foreign investor gaining access. Many foreign investors rightly questioned why they should invest in a country Iranians themselves refused to invest in.

This acute absence of investment, domestic or otherwise, meant that the Islamic Republic of Iran was becoming the extractive state par excellence. Resources were extracted and profits shipped abroad to avoid scrutiny and taxation. The volatility and opaqueness encouraged by a mercantile mentality in turn ensured that the best way to secure one's income was to deposit it abroad, weakening the currency and gradually impoverishing the state.

This weakening of the currency, of course, maximized the purchasing power of those who had access to hard currency, further encouraging deposits to stay abroad. It was a perverse and highly destructive situation. Later, as international sanctions mounted, this opaqueness would be turned into a necessity and a virtue, but this particular imperative long predated the sanctions regime. It was not long before Khatami was describing the economy as sick, and he was quick to discover that there was little enthusiasm for the surgery he prescribed.

Matters became acute when Khatami spearheaded a landslide election victory in the parliament in 2000, clearing away any legislative block to his programme of reform. The victory was all the more surprising because, a year earlier, he had faced his first serious political crisis with the student uprisings of 1999, in which his attempt to navigate a median path had potentially damaged his credibility with the key student constituency that had supported him. But the government report into the protests had not shied away from criticizing the security forces for provoking them, and a number of officials were arrested.

The Judiciary, very much in hard-line control, did little to pursue effective prosecutions, but a clear signal had been sent that the government had no intention of whitewashing controversial incidents. Even more striking was Khatami's swift dismissal of the none too subtle threat of intervention from members of the IRGC, with the retort that Khomeini himself had instructed the Guards (and indeed any of the military) to stay out of politics.

It represented an ominous portent, even if presently unrealized, of the IRGC's enthusiasm for political intervention, and senior members voiced their belief that, as guardians of the Revolution, their role was to defend it from enemies without and within.

For a brief moment in 2000, however, reformists were in a state of elation, seemingly unaware that, like their intellectual forebears in 1906, a vicious reaction was about to set in. By the end of that year, they were in receipt of two shocks. The first was an attempted assassination of the strategic mastermind behind the reform movement, Saeed Hajjarian, a former intelligence official with a keen eye on the realities of politics, shot at close range and left as a paraplegic.

The second was the explicit intervention of the Supreme Leader Ayatollah Khamenei in the legislative process by blocking the passage of a bill liberalizing the press. As the ambitious legislative programme stuttered to a halt, it soon became apparent that the Leader's vote outweighed all others and, as excitement gave way to despair, some could not avoid the metaphor of Hajjarian's failed assassination. The idea of reform was far from dead, but it had for all practical purposes been paralysed.

7
Crisis of Authority
(2001–2009)

Khatami would win a second term handsomely in 2001. His popularity, much to the consternation of the hardliners, remained high, even if some were voting for him to avoid the unpalatable alternative. But his second term proved a brutal contest for power and his room for manoeuvre was progressively constrained. The hardliners, who increasingly identified themselves as new conservatives or 'Principle-ists' (a mistranslation of 'fundamentalist', on the basis that they understood that term to mean someone who stuck to their fundamentals/principles), were getting ready to deliver their *coup de grâce* through electoral manipulation and the introduction of the joker in their pack, the man of the people who would finally consign reformism to the dustbin. This would, of course, be an exercise in populism rather than democracy, a distinction they did not fully comprehend, and the man to deliver it would be the hitherto unknown teacher at the Basij (Islamic militia) university, Mahmoud Ahmadinejad.

The Twilight of Reformism

Ahmadinejad claimed an authentic revolutionary pedigree, having served in the IRGC during the war. The absence of any evidence of this was explained by the fact that he had apparently served in covert operations, a suggestion that was later challenged by those who claimed that, on the contrary, he had served behind the lines in logistics. Nonetheless, his overt piety and fascination with the Hidden Imam, combined with a deft popular touch, had brought him to the attention of the Principle-ist establishment, including members of the Supreme Leader's office. With formal, if discreet, backing, Ahmadinejad's rise was inexorable. In 2003, he was elected mayor of Tehran on risible turnout. People rarely paid attention to local elections but, with disillusion setting in, turnout was even more suppressed, favouring the hard-line factions who could easily mobilize their support.

Then, in 2004, just to be certain of victory, over 3,000 reformist candidates were barred from running, in an extraordinary vetting operation by the Guardian Council, ensuring that the elections would be 'won' by Principle-ists. Rafsanjani, who had taken the fateful step of giving the Guardian Council these powers, for which they had to provide no accounting or reason, declined to comment, since he too had tired of reformists who had ceaselessly berated him for his corruption. More damning was the absence of any European comment on this blatantly rigged election.

Having initiated talks on Iran's nuclear programme and convinced themselves that concrete results could only be achieved with those 'conservatives' who held the real power, comment was withheld. The trouble was that the 'conservatives' coming into power were to neither Rafsanjani's nor the West's liking.

Indication that this might be the case was soon to be in evidence. One of the great opportunities for détente with the West had been missed in the aftermath of 9/11. Khatami, who had always been open to better relations and indeed regarded some form of international stability as essential to the political and economic development of Iran itself, now saw an opportunity in the tragedy that had unfolded on that fateful September morning. As it became clear that the culprits were not Shia or in any way associated with Iran, Khatami moved, despite some internal criticism, to offer condolences and support, and by all accounts his administration offered valuable intelligence on Afghanistan to the Americans. There was no love lost between Iran and the Taleban and, indeed, a few years earlier, Iran had even contemplated going to war against them (scouring the 1857 Treaty of Paris for the legal justification). Now this task would be achieved by the United States, with which Iran found a fortuitous coincidence of interest. Sadly, the Bush administration failed to seize the opportunity for a cautious diplomatic revolution and, during the State of the Union address in 2002, labelled Iran as part of an axis of evil, along with North Korea and Iraq.

This attack proved to be another nail in the coffin carefully crafted for Khatami by his hard-line opponents, who taunted Khatami for his naïvety in trusting the Americans. Still, with the invasion of Iraq in 2003, the Iranians found themselves supporting the overthrow of their nemesis and, in the immediate aftermath, moved to provide some of the social and economic architecture that the invasion and occupation had recklessly removed. There were signs that, for all the friction that existed, the coalition welcomed Iran's input. Others in the region of course did not, and worried with some justification that the Iranian assistance would be difficult to remove.

Their fears proved justified with the change of political climate in Iran. With the new parliament now in place and the Khatami administration biding its time before its departure from office, the Iranian presence in Iraq was handed to the IRGC. The Iranians had argued, with understandable justification, that their aim in Iraq was to prevent a military threat emerging from that country again. But now, with the US menace dissipating as it became bogged down in a guerrilla war, Iranian strategy switched to a proactive mode whereby it sought to accelerate the US withdrawal. It is from 2004 that the Allied coalition found itself contending against an Iranian presence that was supplying weapons and Improvised Explosive Devices (IEDs) to its Iraqi opponents.

It is important here to recognize the ideological shift that was taking place in Iran, with the move from those who had prioritized the republic, to those who saw the Revolution of 1979 in a purist, even puritanical, Islamist mode. Whereas reformist and traditional conservatives like Rafsanjani tended to see the Revolution as part of an intellectual evolution that could be traced back to 1906 – one might quibble on the details, but the inheritance was clear – the Principle-ists viewed the Revolution through an exclusively Islamic lens which dismissed 1906 as a Western-imposed distraction. What the Islamic Revolution was fundamentally about was about imposing, for the first time, true Islam, and ridding the Islamic world of the 'Crusaders'. This was thus a global struggle of some historical depth that had more in common with other radical Islamic movements than with Iranian history. In this sense, the Islamic Revolution was not correcting the aberration of the Pahlavi period and returning Iran to its traditional foundations, but engaging in a radical diversion and departure of its own. The IRGC was the armed wing of this struggle, but the intellectual and political heart lay with the radical clergy and the office of the Supreme Leader.

Ahmadinejad and the Triumph of Populism

It took some time for people to appreciate the shift that had taken place, but the election of Mahmoud Ahmadinejad to the presidency in 2005 provided the clearest indication of what was going on. Ahmadinejad's victory was in part stage-managed insofar as it was unlikely he would have made it to the run-off. Few people took him seriously and, while his stint as mayor of Tehran had brought him some valuable publicity, his achievements seemed largely presentational. (Ahmadinejad's supporters claimed, for example, that he had been voted international 'mayor of the year', in what proved to be an internet poll of dubious validity.) He clearly had the popular touch and, in the context of a political establishment that seemed increasingly disconnected from the travails of ordinary people, he enjoyed the appeal of the insurgent.

With the first stage having been carefully manipulated, Ahmadinejad found himself contending against a returning Rafsanjani whose lacklustre campaign betrayed a dangerous hubris. Confident of victory, Rafsanjani found himself up against not only the deep State, but the Iranian tendency to give the establishment a good kicking. Rafsanjani had never been a political campaigner, even if he had been an effective political operator.

Disdainful of Ahmadinejad, he singularly failed to take him seriously and allowed himself to be painted as the face of a corrupt establishment. Ahmadinejad's campaign, meanwhile, had learnt all the modern media tricks of the Khatami campaign some eight years before, turning to social media and the Internet to connect with people. Much to the horror of the traditional conservative establishment, to say nothing of reformists, he triumphed in the second round.

Like other insurgents who have seemingly triumphed against insuperable odds, Ahmadinejad was quick to dismiss the practical help he had enjoyed in securing the presidency. Instead, he and his followers were swift to interpret his 'miraculous' rise to power as Providential, and proceeded accordingly. The hardline establishment was naturally elated that its man had won an electoral victory, consigning, as they saw it, reformism to history, but little did they appreciate just how mercurial Ahmadinejad would become.

On one important level, he delivered, exploiting an advantage none of his predecessors enjoyed: an inflated oil price. Ahmadinejad spent generously but simultaneously dismantled what remained of the auditing bodies of the government, the most egregious being the abolition of the Plan and Budget Organization, which had been in existence since the 1940s. Without systematic oversight, he began the wholesale transfer of assets from the 'republic' to the revolutionary institutions, expanding the remit for the revolutionary organizations, notably the IRGC, to engage in commercial activities.

Some have assessed that Iran's oil revenue by value in the eight years of Ahmadinejad's presidency exceeded by some margin the total earned since the discovery of oil, concluding that, in the absence of transparency, some $800 bn of revenue had gone missing. It hadn't, of course. Some people became enormously rich just as the State bankrupted itself. While oil revenues were high, however, much of the systemic damage remained hidden, disguised as it was by the lavish expenditure of what amounted in reality to patronage.

What was equally striking was the shift in ideological worldview that was taking place among the political establishment. Ahmadinejad was a product of the Principle-ist movement, whose members regarded themselves as the guardians of the purity of the Islamic Revolution. These were not conservatives in the traditional understanding of the term. Eschewing any link with Rafsanjani and his supporters, whom they regarded as corrupt, they identified with an austere reading of the Revolution and its ideas, authentic and puritanical. These new conservatives believed they had finally rescued the Revolution from the misguided policies of Rafsanjani and the heresy of Khatami, for this political movement defined itself in acutely religious terms, seeing itself as part of a 'culture' war in which its opponents were not simply rivals or competitors but very much beyond the pale.

It was in this period that Iranian political society was divided into three distinct parts: us, you, and them. The inner sanctum of true believers was identified as 'us'; those on the margins, trusted acolytes and useful idiots, would be defined as 'you': never part of the elect, they nonetheless served a useful purpose and with some effort might make it into the elect. 'Them' represented the great mass of unbelievers, not simply in the political order of the day but in an acutely religious sense that would become explicit during the Green Movement uprisings in 2009. For now, these distinctions remained unspoken if under-stood, and Ahmadinejad enthusiastically engaged in his role, as the populist-in-chief turned his attention towards disrupting the global order.

Validated by his election triumph, and awash with oil money, Ahmadinejad turned his attention to the global stage. Widely mocked for his fixation with the Hidden Imam – with whom he felt he had an intimate connection – Ahmadinejad would pander to the con-viction that his government was that of the Hidden Imam by conspicuously leaving a space at the cabinet table in case the Hidden Imam decided to reveal him-self and join them. For the 'true believers', along with those with a penchant for superstition, such behav-iour reflected Ahmadinejad's deep piety. For many others, including some senior and somewhat weary clerics, this was a theatre of the absurd.

For Ahmadinejad, needless to say, only the global stage would suffice. It was not sufficient for him to talk to Iranians, he had to take his mission to a global audience, and his honeymoon with a foreign press corps that was at first curious proved short-lived. During his first visit to the UN General Assembly in New York in September 2005 he gave full expression to his religious obsession to a bewildered audience, later claiming in a meeting with a senior cleric that the delegates were so impressed with his speech that they did not blink for half an hour, such was the awe with which they greeted his words. He added for good measure that he sensed a green halo around him when he spoke, presumably the presence of the Hidden Imam. Such commentary invited ridicule, not least in Iran itself, and even the cleric was moved to comment enigmatically that people should avoid misleading others.

Far from heeding such warnings, Ahmadinejad showed himself to have a remarkably thick skin, basking in the controversy he was causing in the belief that he was speaking truth to power. If the Western press corps were initially entertained by what they considered to be an exercise in naïve buffoonery, his later comments about the Holocaust and the State of Israel were to change the tone altogether.

It was perhaps in its international ambitions that the reinvigorated ideology of the Principle-ists gained its most fulsome and explicit expression. If they felt that they had to prepare Iran for the return of the Hidden Imam and the new order, so too were they compelled to address the incongruities of the international order, established – as they saw, unjustly – in the aftermath of the Second World War. This 'unjust' order, founded in the interest of the West (for some reason, Russia and China were omitted from this), was founded on the basis of a lie – the Holocaust – which gave rise to that emblematic injustice, the State of Israel. The way to undo this was therefore to speak truth to power and expose the lie.

Whereas previous presidents had defined their opposition to Israel on the injustice being perpetrated against the Palestinians, Ahmadinejad took it a step further, regarding the elimination of the State of Israel as being the key to unlocking the entire international order, in preparation for the return of the Hidden Imam. Much ink has been spilt by pundits about quite what Ahmadinejad said or meant when he referred to Israel being 'wiped from the pages of history', but a cursory glance at the supporting documents and statements (an Iranian missile draped in a flag saying Israel must be destroyed) left little room for interpretation. If Khatami had condemned the Holocaust, Ahmadinejad urged further 'research', while his supporters simply proclaimed it a hoax. His frequent proclamations in this regard served notice that matters had changed, but with the focus on Ahmadinejad, few people appreciated that he was simply the visible tip of an ideological iceberg.

Ahmadinejad was merely the public and most vulgar face of an ideology that was being developed around the person of the Supreme Leader. Its aim was an Islamic State rather than an Islamic Republic, in which the focus of everyone's attention would be the Supreme Leader in his capacity as the deputy of the Hidden Imam, while the latter remained in occultation. Khamenei had long had to contend with the disdain of many senior, old-school clerics who had viewed his elevation to the leadership with barely disguised contempt.

Now many were dead, and others had been sidelined, while Khamenei himself spent lavishly from the State coffers – replenished generously by

Ahmadinejad's diversion of funds – to create an extensive network of patronage. He also sought to create a new sacral loyalty to his own person as the intermediary with the Hidden Imam, by heavily investing in and developing the shrine in Jamkaran, south of Tehran, much beloved by Ahmadinejad and his followers – the location of a well from which some believed the Hidden Imam would emerge.

By encouraging the development of this shrine, Khamenei sought to divert pilgrims from more traditional sites and to emphasize his own sacral associations. Ahmadinejad, needless to say, obliged by conspicuously attending the shrine and dropping a missive from the waiting 'Imam' down the well. More traditional Shias were contemptuous of such performance art, which they regarded as the promotion of superstition among the gullible masses.

Where Ahmadinejad went wrong was in his growing self-belief and the conceit that he was the ideologue rather than simply the messenger – that he was not simply the vulgar expression intended to shore up the authority of the Supreme Leader, but the source of emulation himself. Intoxicated by his apparent popularity, he drew on nationalist and religious symbols with eclectic abandon, even co-opting Cyrus the Great to his cause in a manner which drew unfavourable comparisons with the last Shah. For all that, Khamenei could not resist suggesting that Ahmadinejad's government was the greatest since the Constitutional Revolution.

The Green Movement

Matters, however, came to a head in 2009 when Ahmadinejad, now very much sitting on the crest of a wave of his own imagination, decided to run for re-election. Keen on a high turnout and a solid vote to consolidate the triumph of 2005, the regime miscalculated badly. Determined to engineer a landslide election victory for Ahmadinejad on a scale that would banish the idea of reform and its iconic leader, Mohammad Khatami, to the margins of political life forever, the authorities decided to relax the strictures on campaigning.

Political campaigns in Iran had traditionally been quite austere and tightly controlled, at least in terms of the time allocated. Political activity might be energized for a month but that was about the most the regime could cope with. Now convinced of Ahmadinejad's ability to ride the popular wave back to a stunning re-election, the regime decided on a lengthy campaign which would also serve to showcase Iran's Islamic democracy to the wider world.

Hubris ensured that they failed to see the challenge coming their way. Khatami was urged to stand but, with his nerves badly frayed by his previous experience, decided to sit this one out. The focus of reformists turned to the former Prime Minister during the war years, Mir Hossein Mousavi, whom the regime was happy to contend with because, for all his apparent competence, he lacked the verve and chutzpah of

Ahmadinejad. Journalists who were invited to observe the elections expressed themselves impressed by the energy on the streets, but regime stalwarts were soon expressing concern at what they had unleashed and whether Ahmadinejad would be able to ride the tiger after all.

If the authorities were content with Ahmadinejad's bombastic performance in the televised debates, they were less than impressed with the ground operation being mobilized by Mousavi's supporters, with a vast network of street organizers ready to bring out the vote throughout the country. Some 48 hours before the election, the authorities moved to re-establish control over an electoral performance that was in danger of producing a result they did not want.

Elections were traditionally run by the Ministry of the Interior. But, on previous occasions, the Ministry had found itself at odds with the other organs of election oversight, such as the hard-line Guardian Council, ensuring that some competitive negotiation always took place. On this occasion, Ahmadinejad's ministry was working very much hand in glove with the Guardian Council. It was partly in recognition of this reality that the Mousavi campaign had established such a sophisticated ground operation, organizing their own monitors to ensure that, if the worst came to the worst, they might be able to embarrass the authorities into minimizing their own interventions. With foreign journalists swarming the streets of Tehran, this might be a possibility.

As it happened, however, the authorities decided they didn't want to take any chances, moving substantial security forces into the capital, arresting key leaders of the reform movement on the night before the vote and turning the Ministry of the Interior into a fortress, on the pretext that 'seditionists' were about to cause trouble. Most perniciously, the authorities put it about that the government was going to trial a new form of electronic vote counting which would speed up the count considerably. Just how fast was to surprise many, as results were prematurely announced on a hard-line website before the vote had actually ended. Swiftly removed, the results were nonetheless incrementally announced within hours of the end of the vote, with the percentage win for Ahmadinejad staying strangely consistent throughout the night. Indeed, by the early hours of the morning, far in advance of previous election counts, Ahmadinejad had to all intents and purposes won.

Voters woke up the next morning with the results seemingly finalized. Without waiting for the Guardian Council to confirm the vote – a procedure which on previous occasions would normally take a few days – Khamenei announced himself greatly satisfied with the result and the huge endorsement this had apparently given his favoured candidate. To those who questioned the rapidity of the count came the answer that the new electronic system had worked wonders. But voters wondered how exactly the system had worked when the system of submitting handwritten ballots – a system clearly vulnerable to manipulation – was still in practice.

There was as yet no such thing as a secret ballot in Iranian elections. Voters would enter the voting station with their ID, pick up a ballot paper, check the number of the candidate on the list (often different from their ranking on the list) and then hand-write that name on the form before submitting it in the ballot box. The clarity of writing in Persian can vary for every individual, which allowed those tallying the votes to often dismiss or misread votes according to preference.

After all the boasting of the new electronic counting system, the uninitiated might have assumed that these ballots were counted electronically, but such a sophisticated OCR (Optical Character Recognition) system did not exist in Iran and the ballots were taken, as normal, to individual homes of designated counters (another idiosyncrasy of the Iranian system) where the votes were tallied and then the numbers input into a computer system which would collate all the numbers at the Ministry of the Interior. The actual procedure for the counting of votes had therefore not changed at all.

It did not take long for protesters to take to the streets, as the campaign organization switched to organizing nationwide protests. The regime found itself confronting the most extensive protests in a generation, and certainly the most serious challenge to its authority since 1979. Moreover, it faced the prospect of the protests being observed by the cohort of foreign journalists still in situ. Even Mousavi was surprised at the level of the anger he witnessed, with crowds reaching, by the government's own estimation, some 3 million people. Slogans that had hitherto been considered taboo, against the Supreme Leader and his family, were now becoming widespread, as were chants against Russia, widely regarded as supporting the regime.

As journalists' visas lapsed and they returned home, so the regime began to take more aggressive action. First, they arrested Mousavi and other leaders, and then, following the now characteristic speech by the Supreme Leader announcing that he could not be held responsible for the actions of his security forces, those forces were unleashed into the crowds. By all accounts, it proved to be a very bloody affair. Official accounts that less than 100 people died in the months of protests which followed cannot be relied upon, in large part because there were few means of impartial observation, particularly outside Tehran.

But what was striking was how long it took to suppress the protests, which were better organized and more socially networked than anyone had imagined. They were, to be sure, organized through mobile phones rather than Twitter, as some argued, but they were organized and far from a mob. The regime resorted to terror tactics, the arbitrary destruction of property and random attacks on people, even bystanders, to induce social anxiety and fear, but the attempts of the regime to define their opponents as 'heretics' were meeting with some opposition among senior clerics increasingly concerned at the direction of travel the authorities were taking.

By mid-summer, with the protests still in full flow – Ahmadinejad had decried the protesters as mere dust and dirt, in a speech even his supporters considered unwise – the leading ideologue of the Principle-ist faction, Ayatollah Mesbah Yazdi, had stated that obedience to Ahmadinejad was the equivalent to obedience to God and, furthermore, that belief in the *velayat-e faqih* (Guardianship of the Jurist) should henceforth be considered one of the pillars of the faith and the mark of a true Muslim. Even hard-line papers found the first statement concerning and quickly withdrew it, but Mesbah Yazdi's claim was that the new order was sacred, and all those who protested against it were waging war against God and therefore beyond the protection of the law. As revelations of torture and brutality surfaced, it became all too apparent what this meant in practice.

It was an astonishing development that shone a light into the deepest recesses of Principle-ist ideology. Ideas that hitherto might not have extended beyond the inner circle were now being made public and, while largely ignored by observers overseas, laid bare the direction of travel now being followed. If the republic was not yet dead, it was not long for this world. The rationale behind the notion of obedience was very simply that Khamenei was the representative of the Hidden Imam, with all his powers, and once he had validated the President, the latter received these powers as an extension of the Leader's charisma.

Just as the Leader was accountable to no one but God, so too was the President and, taken to its logical conclusion, much of the government. The people existed to confirm by acclamation, little else. Senior clerics who criticized these developments were swiftly sidelined. But there was one whom they had not reckoned with, and that was the ageing Ayatollah Montazeri, the one-time successor to Khomeini who had been disbarred on account of his earlier criticism of human rights abuses.

Montazeri had been released from house arrest on the basis that he was now so old he could do no harm. But as the protests continued, he found his voice, and arguably the most serious threat to the regime occurred in what was to prove the twilight of the protests in December 2009 as Montazeri positioned himself as a leading clerical opponent of the regime. His presence appeared to re-energize the protests and give it religious validity. But then, with a suddenness that shocked his followers and was regarded as Providential by the regime, Montazeri died. The shock was so widespread that the wind was dramatically taken out of the protesters' sails. The protests petered out.

The authorities moved quickly to root out the dissent in a suppression so systematic it was to prove, in time, counterproductive. Show trials proceeded on a scale not seen since the early days of the Revolution, with levels of absurdity that were unmatched. Obsessed as they were with the use of the works of Max Weber in reformist articles, the long dead German sociologist found himself on trial in Tehran for sedition. If the protests had been crushed, the long-term malaise that was infecting the regime was now on display for all to see. This was a deep political crisis that would not easily be resolved.

The year 2009 was a pivotal moment in the history of the Islamic Republic: the year when the new direction of travel was confirmed and when people realized, slowly but surely, that reform was no longer a realistic possibility. The logic of that conclusion had yet to be realized, but there was a clear gulf emerging between the State and its people. The 'Guardian Jurist', who was meant to have provided ethical oversight, was becoming a monarch in all but name – there was a growing belief that he intended his son Mojtaba to succeed him – with few if any constitutional restrictions on his power.

But this was a monarch with powers that would far exceed those enjoyed by Iran's traditional rulers. This was a sacral monarchy that held itself accountable to God alone, in what appeared to be an attempt to overturn what were proving to be the modest achievements of the Constitutional Revolution. The Pahlavi monarchs had paid lip service to the constitutional limitations on their power that had been imposed by the Revolution of 1906, but they still believed in their role as 'national' monarchs serving national interests.

If pre-constitutional monarchs aspired to absolute power, they rarely achieved it in practice because of the realities of exercising that power. The new 'Guardians' also faced practical limitations, but the tools of the modern state and the advance of technology ensured that many of the traditional restrictions were being steadily reduced. Their ability to penetrate society was constrained by their own inefficiency and corruption but, with vast oil wealth, extensive patronage and a new cult of the Supreme Leader, many of the accoutrements of the 'Republic' were proving to be surplus to requirements. Bodies that were intended to represent a clear separation of powers were being reduced to ciphers, and even the parliament, that iconic achievement of 1906, was described by some recalcitrant deputies as a mere extension of the Leader's office.

The triumph of 2009 was, however, illusory. Power had been restored but at the cost of wider authority, and more astute observers were aware of the problems they faced. One notable exception was Ahmadinejad, who regarded the crisis of 2009 as particular to Khamenei rather than himself, an exercise in narcissistic unawareness that was to heighten the tensions between his government and the Supreme Leader in his final term as the regime turned to deal with another looming crisis, that of Iran's nuclear programme.

On the one hand, it proved a useful international diversion with which to unify the country. But poorly handled, as Ahmadinejad seemed intent on it being, it could also add an international dimension to the domestic crisis facing the regime, leading to increased isolation and sanctions which would add further to the regime's burgeoning crisis of authority.

8
Paranoid State
(2010–)

The Islamic Revolution of 1979 had positioned itself as a popular revolution that sought to fulfil the promise of over a century of political struggle to establish a modern state with the rule of law in which citizens enjoyed rights. It defined itself against what it saw as the tyranny of 2,500 years of monarchy, and delivered a 'republic' with Islamic oversight. From its very inception, there were tensions between the republican and Islamic aspects of the new constitution, and between those who felt that the Revolution had been fought to fulfil the promise of 1906 and those who believed that it had inaugurated a radical new age of Islamic awakening, for which the 'republic' was merely a transitory phase towards the kingdom of God on earth.

Those who believed in the Republic held sway until 2005, struggling to contend with the reactionary forces which surrounded the Supreme Leader. From the end of Khatami's presidency, they were on the defensive, launching what proved to be their swansong in 2009. Their ruthless suppression tore the heart out of the reform movement and convinced many that internal reform towards a republic that worked for its citizens was a forlorn hope. Those who believed in an Islamic

State around the autocracy of the Supreme Leader were now in the ascendancy and, far from believing they had to win the other side over, they simply opted to dismiss them as beyond the pale.

The Republic was finished and there was no point arguing about it. Legitimacy had to be sought elsewhere. People could choose to buy into the new religious order or not, as the case may be, but another more fruitful route might be to deploy nationalism and to show that the State could still defend Iran's national interests. A crisis that might yet be turned into an opportunity was that over Iran's nuclear programme, which had been simmering since 2003.

The Nuclear Negotiations

The international community's attention was drawn towards Iran's nuclear programme in the aftermath of 9/11. It was not that they ignored it beforehand, and even the Shah's ambitions in the 1970s had elicited curiosity from the United States in particular, especially when it became apparent that he sought enrichment capability. Those were, of course, different times and Iran was ostensibly an ally, but, more importantly, nuclear power was viewed differently. Be that as it may, with the fall of the Shah, the nuclear programme was shut down on the basis that it had been a colossal waste of money and an imperialist plot to recycle Iran's money westwards. Scientists were imprisoned and the programme mothballed.

Partly as a consequence of the vulnerabilities revealed by the Iran–Iraq War, along with a need to show industrial and scientific competency, the programme was reinvigorated in the 1980s. As with much else in the Islamic Republic, its nuclear policy was simply lifted from the 1970s and now misapplied to a new era. It accelerated in the aftermath of the war. But, of course, circumstances had changed. Iran's economic position was no longer as strong, it had turned on its Western allies, but the international attitude to nuclear power had also shifted dramatically since the halcyon days of the 1970s. None of this seems to have deterred the officials in the Islamic Republic as they became intoxicated with the notion of scientific progress which would show emphatically that 'Islam' was not contradictory to science.

But in lifting the programme from the 1970s, Iran failed to adapt the arguments in favour of establishing a nuclear industry beyond those the Shah had put forward. The public justification, as in the 1970s, was the diversification of energy supply, but this case was even weaker in the 1990s and 2000s because the plans would not have contributed much to Iran's energy needs by then, when the population had more than doubled. Moreover, the Shah had argued that much of Iran's hydrocarbon resources would be depleted, hence the need to develop nuclear power as part of a wider diversification of energy sources. He had, for example, boasted about developing solar power, for which he was much mocked by Khomeini, who wondered aloud how energy could be procured from the sun.

With little development or exploitation of Iran's hydrocarbon resources after the Revolution and the discovery of vast gas fields – Iran had the second-largest reserves of natural gas outside Russia – this argument seemed less effective. The need to establish an industry also seemed to carry less weight, simply because the cost of doing so was by all accounts prohibitive. Even when the Shah discussed this, Western officials noted that few countries were either able or willing to establish a self-sufficient industry, because it was simply inefficient to do so. Far better to be expert in particular areas. But then the Shah was awash with cash. The Islamic Republic was far from rich.

In one area, of course, worries persisted, and that was regarding enrichment technology and the pursuit of weaponization. The Shah had always demurred on this question, but his overwhelming regional military superiority calmed a number of Western anxieties. He may go for breakout as South Asia had done, but there was certainly no urgency on his part. The Islamic Republic likewise pursued an ambiguous position on this question, but unlike the Shah they were not basking in military superiority and, on the contrary, had suffered the depredations of an eight-year war. Given the incongruities of the economic case, it was not surprising suspicions were raised.

Iran, realizing that it had found a cause to which most Iranians, in Iran or the diaspora, could attach themselves, portrayed its nuclear policy as one of grievance and rights denied. This became a matter of principle and Western double standards, and in seeking to draw an unfettered line straight back to the Shah, studiously ignoring the obvious impact of the Islamic Revolution, they sought to present this as a distinctly 'Iranian' problem, not one particular to the Islamic Republic. In presenting this narrative, Western incoherence played into their hands, but, as always, the Iranians tended to overstate the hand they had.

Ahmadinejad certainly did not hold back, boasting about the developments in Iran's enrichment technology and looking forward to a time when 'industrial-scale' enrichment would allow Iran to sell enriched uranium 'commercially' abroad. Quite apart from being economic nonsense, such ambitions were anathema to the West, and unsettling to both the Chinese and the Russians. But so alarmed were they by these developments that they relegated other matters to the margins, focusing almost exclusively on Iran's nuclear progress.

For Iran's hardliners, this proved to be another benefit of Ahmadinejad's flamboyant nuclear diplomacy. Iran's transition from an Islamic Republic to an Islamic 'security' State was proceeding right under the noses of the West, whose focus on nuclear matters blinded them to the wider political hinterland which was in many ways equally, if not more, problematic. The West had concluded that a resolution to the nuclear impasse would release tensions and open the door to liberalization. But they had erroneously accepted the argument that Iran's problems were international rather than domestic in origin – that the nuclear impasse was a cause rather than a symptom of a wider political malaise.

When President Obama took office in January 2009, he made clear his determination to turn the page with the Islamic Republic, to settle outstanding disputes and restore relations. This had to start with the question of Iran's nuclear programme, and to initiate proceedings Obama decided to write directly to the Supreme Leader offering reassurance about Western policy and seeking talks. If, traditionally, it had been the President who dealt with international relations, Obama's approach was a recognition of growing political realities, but it also served to hasten the process by which the Supreme Leader became the hegemon in practice as well as theory.

Obama had managed to convince himself that his predecessors' failures with regard to Iran were largely, though not exclusively, a consequence of their failure to understand the country. US–Iran relations were in sum held back by a misunderstanding that could be resolved with a bit of open-mindedness and empathy. It was US interventions in the past, not least the coup in 1953, which had created the mistrust, and the United States had to be cognizant of this and tread carefully.

In taking this approach, the Obama administration was defining policy almost exclusively through the attitudes and debates in the Washington beltway, with little reference to developments in Iran itself. Had they bothered to look at Iran, they would have soon appreciated that official affectation for Mosaddeq was another example of performance art. Few members of the Principle-ist elite were remotely interested in Mosaddeq's secular constitutionalism. But they understood his value in promoting guilt in the West. When the protests erupted in 2009, Obama was nonplussed, reacted cautiously and basically served notice, to all who could hear, that a nuclear settlement, and nuclear security, trumped the rights of individual Iranians. It was a message that was bitterly resented by Iran's protesters and one which Obama later came to regret.

Indeed, as the protests waned, Ahmadinejad moved quickly to re-establish the negotiations which had been continuing now for several years. Initial attempts to reach a resolution in 2003 and 2004 had fallen flat following the change in government in Iran, while Ahmadinejad's grandstanding, coinciding as it did with US difficulties in Iraq – which Ahmadinejad and his IRGC allies sought to exacerbate – resulted in the talks stalling. The US at this stage refused to be directly involved in the talks, which ensured a frustrating trilateral negotiation in which the Europeans (Britain, France and Germany) had to consult with the United States before any proposals could be tabled. With Obama's willingness to engage, the talks gained new momentum and seriousness, and with the Iranian file having been sent by the IAEA to the UN

Security Council – a move Ahmadinejad dismissed as worthless – all members of the Security Council plus Germany (P5+1) were now directly involved in the negotiations.

Ahmadinejad, for his part, could only lap up the international attention, but his enthusiasm for performing on the international stage created more problems than it solved. Quite apart from his extravagant claims, his bombastic pronouncements and somewhat erratic approach made him an unreliable partner. In 2010, even the Russians, who were thought to be the most sympathetic to the Iranian position grew tired of him after he had rejected their proposal and turned to a similar proposal from Turkey, a country that was not even part of the formal negotiating team.

By 2011, the Americans were able to get the P5+1 on board for the most stringent set of financial sanctions to be imposed on Iran. In addition to those imposed by the United States and Europe, sanctions were now imposed by the United Nations and which all members were beholden to follow. Ahmadinejad was resolutely dismissive of what was to come, almost challenging the international community to do its worst. And they did, isolating Iran from the international banking system and imposing an EU embargo on purchases of Iranian oil. The only response came in the form of an assault on the British Embassy in Tehran, ostensibly by students – although many seemed unusually mature – resulting in the ransacking of the embassy and the withdrawal of British diplomats (though not a formal break in relations).

Having contained, if not resolved, the crisis of 2009, the State now found itself financially hide-bound. Far from being a useful diversion which could unify Iranians around a new nationalist cause, the nuclear crisis had added new burdens to a state already creaking under the weight of its own ineptitude. It was striking that, almost immediately, Khamenei circumvented his president and without his knowledge authorized secret talks to begin with the United States, in Oman. The talks, which formally began in 2012, were the clearest indication of the growing irrelevance of the presidency.

Rouhani and the JCPOA

Be that as it may, presentation mattered. Khamenei was aware that Ahmadinejad was a growing problem, not only in dealing with international interlocutors – not least the Russians – but also domestically. With the emergence of the Arab Spring and the outbreak of protests in Syria, Russia was becoming an increasingly important partner for Iran but, more than that, for Iran to be able to have more freedom of action in the region she needed to be free of UN sanctions.

With Ahmadinejad's second term concluding in 2013, Khamenei was determined to replace him with someone more amenable and able to take the negotiations public. Hasan Rouhani, who had once held Iran's nuclear portfolio, was now hailed as the new face of 'moderate' conservatism, although he campaigned very much as a reformist. Supported by both Khatami and Rafsanjani, who found himself ignominiously ruled out of running on account of his advanced age, Rouhani seized the reins of a much debased presidency in 2013. For the regime, Rouhani's victory was a political masterpiece. Not only did it appear to close the door on the crisis of 2009, but it opened up the possibility of constructive negotiations on the nuclear programme.

It is interesting to reflect whether Iran's nuclear programme was important to her as an end in itself, or primarily as a means of leverage. The West had convinced itself that Iran's primary goal was to seek weapons capability, and, while this never seems to have been far from people's minds in Iran, this goal was often tempered by the realization that the 'threat' could bring benefits of its own, not least a Western preoccupation with this matter at the expense of all others, including the country's domestic political and human rights record. This became apparent in the negotiations that followed Rouhani's election victory.

Rouhani was a politician who campaigned in loquacious poetry but governed in dry prose. His promises during the campaign on political liberalization were so grand as to make the impression that Iran was on the verge of a return to 1997 and the Reform ascendancy. That of course was the point, and such was the desperation of his audience that they were only too willing to believe. This was also the case in the West, where, in their enthusiasm to get to a resolution to the nuclear crisis, little attention was paid to the realities of politics.

This was a mistake, because, while Western analysts claimed that a resolution of international tensions would open the possibility to political liberalization – a view encouraged by Rouhani himself – the reality was that Iran's approach to its international relations would be dictated by domestic politics, which were hardening by the day. Certainly, Khamenei's view of the negotiations, couched in heavy distrust of the West, was that any agreement would be limited and purely transactional.

Be that as it may, Rouhani's election in 2013 seemed to augur a new dawn, made all the more dramatic by the fact that few people were aware that the negotiations had already started in earnest a year earlier. By all accounts, even Rouhani was shocked that the Supreme Leader had authorized secret talks with the United States. When the interim Joint Plan of Action (JPOA) was announced later that year, it was not quite the diplomatic revolution that people assumed. Indeed, given the work that had been done, the real question is why it took so long to get to the final Comprehensive agreement two years later.

Part of this was a reflection of the deep mistrust which existed, not between the negotiating teams but between their respective political masters in Tehran and Washington, which, for all the genuine anxieties of selling any deal, also ensured that the process needed to appear pained and protracted. In this, the Iranians had the advantage in knowing that the American lead negotiator, John Kerry, needed a success, and needed it before the end of Obama's second and final term.

This ensured that the Iranians were able to turn the tables on the Americans with regard to the urgency of a resolution, all the more so because the threat of military action, which had been used as a stick with which to pressure the Iranians, was now being used by Kerry to shut down hawkish critics at home. The alternative to agreement, he stressed, was yet another war in the Middle East, which the United States could not afford. Moreover, Kerry frequently reiterated Iranian talking points about the resilience of their economy, and a view began to settle that, because of 1953, the US owed Iran – a view that naturally the Iranians encouraged.

Consequently, freed from such pressures as the Americans argued with themselves, the Iranian negotiating team could proceed at their leisure – though, needless to say, they overplayed their hand in this regard too, not reaching an agreement before the US congressional elections that saw the Democrats lose control of Congress. This meant that any chance the Agreement would be submitted for ratification as a Treaty was now lost.

But there were other important ways in which the US conceded dangerous ground to the Iranians, one notable one being the acknowledgement of what was proving to be a remarkably elusive 'fatwa' that the Supreme Leader was supposed to have issued against nuclear weapons. Anxious to tie the Supreme Leader into the process, it was agreed that, in issuing a verbal statement with regard to the illegality of weapons of mass destruction, the Leader had issued a religious injunction obligatory on all Iranians. Quite apart from flatly contradicting the resolution to the Rushdie fatwa, the United States appeared to be endorsing a view which argued that the Supreme Leader's statements amounted to law, a prerogative that unsurprisingly dismayed many Iranian reformists.

The Joint Comprehensive Plan of Action (JCPOA) was agreed to much fanfare in July 2015. It was predicated on the notion that Iran would receive sanctions relief in return for curtailing its nuclear programme. This sanctions relief would ameliorate Iran's economic crisis and open the door to development, which would in time yield political change – a hypothesis so old, tested and discarded, it remains a wonder that it was so uncritically adopted.

As the Shah, Rafsanjani and others might have said, economic reform in the absence of political reform was unlikely to work, yet Rouhani (and his Western supporters) banked not only on economic reform, but reform catalysed by a change in the *international* economic environment. In the absence of any reform of the political economy at home, no amount of encouragement from Western governments could force business to work or invest in Iran.

But the situation was made considerably worse by the flaws which existed in the Agreement. Quite apart from its asymmetric nature – Iran had to address Western concerns before any sanctions relief would be delivered – its failure to address any other issues, notably regional tensions, led to heightened Iranian interference, not least with its newfound ally Russia in Syria.

The most egregious sin of omission as far as the Iranian negotiators were concerned was the failure to remove US primary sanctions, including a bar on using the dollar. This failure to understand the realities of global finance after 2008 basically pre-cluded any bank from engaging in business related to Iran. One of the absurdities of the Agreement was the reality of a divided US position, with the State Department urging economic engagement swiftly fol-lowed by Treasury officials warning businesses to do their 'due diligence'.

The final flaw – though one that few could have foreseen – was in pursuing the JCPOA as an Agreement rather than a Treaty, ratified by Congress. That President Obama could not get any such Agreement through Congress should have served as a warning of the problems that would lie ahead as far as the US was concerned, but the functioning of the Agreement relied very much on the incumbent in the White House and, even if Hillary Clinton had won the election in 2016, the approach to the Agreement would have tightened.

As it was, she was defeated by Donald Trump, who had already served notice that he would abandon the Agreement. The stupidity of his abrupt withdrawal in 2018 was not so much that he sabotaged the Agreement – it was already struggling – but that he refocused attention on the United States as the disruptor and drove a wedge between it and the Europeans.

For Khamenei, of course, Trump's withdrawal was a godsend. It proved America's unreliability, ensured that UN sanctions were unlikely to return, and diverted attention away from his broader plans. However, what the Iranians had miscalculated once again was the impact of Trump's maximum-pressure policy, which saw a range of US sanctions reimposed and/or tightened against Iran. It soon became apparent that, if politically isolated, as far as economic power was concerned America remained the elephant in the room.

For Rouhani, the outcome of the JCPOA proved to be a false dawn. Enthused by the initial success, he had toured the West on an apparent shopping spree which only served to expose the limitations of the Agreement but, perhaps more strikingly, the absence of any economic strategy. In his much lauded attempt to replenish Iran's civilian airline stocks, Rouhani found that banks were unwilling to lend Iran the money to make the outsized purchases of Boeing and Airbus aircraft he sought. But criticism emerged internally, from economists complaining that Rouhani's ambitions bore no relation to Iran's needs or capabilities. Iran lacked the infrastructure to cope with the purchase of the huge Airbus A380 and certainly did not have the market to warrant such purchases. The Iranian view seemed to be that other airlines would simply relinquish routes.

Such incongruities afflicted much of Rouhani's domestic policy, which simply failed to deliver. His similarly much vaunted attempt to establish a citizens' charter fell flat when lawyers realized that any 'rights' would be subject to Islamic laws and sensibilities. The populace soon got the measure of their new smiling President and, while there was general satisfaction at the reaching of an agreement in 2015, its failure to deliver tangible results soon turned that satisfaction to resignation and despair.

Rouhani was successfully re-elected in 2017, in large part because his opponent was the notorious member of the death committee from 1988, the mid-level cleric Ebrahim Raisi. Raisi, the archetypal technocrat and loyalist, had gradually risen through the ranks of the Judiciary and had been appointed the head of one of the largest and wealthiest religious shrines in Mashhad. Some considered that Khamenei was grooming him for the succession and had urged him to stand in the election to boost his public profile. Raisi, for his part, had never denied being part of the death committee, but instead took pride that he had always been ready to take tough decisions. For the majority of the electorate, such pride was a leap too far, and Rouhani was returned with a comfortable majority.

But the populace were proving restless. Even before Trump's withdrawal from the JCPOA, protests had emerged, with demonstrations in the north-eastern city of Mashhad. Some conjectured that these had been encouraged by hardliners to weaken Rouhani, but, if so, it proved a reckless strategy and copycat protests developed. These, however, were a preview of the eruption of discontent in 2019, this time in the south of the country where the State's failure to invest in proper water management had left many people without clean running water.

The protests proved to be among the more serious faced by the Islamic Republic, certainly since 2009, and it took a concerted effort to suppress them. Amnesty International estimated that some 300 people were killed, but other assessments placed the figure much higher at around 1,500. As usual, out of sight and on the peripheries of the country, the State imposed the harshest retribution.

Critics were quick to complain about what appeared to be a shoot-to-kill policy and, in a remarkable admission during a television interview, the Minister of the Interior justified the killing on the claim of an existential threat facing the Islamic Republic. The Minister argued that the protesters were showing increasing ingenuity in their ability to attack infrastructure, which if successful would cripple the State's ability to deliver food and fuel. In justifying the crack down, the Minister inadvertently exposed the real vulnerabilities faced by the State.

This was made all the more apparent by a series of security breaches, ostensibly carried out by the Israelis but which many believed could not have been achieved without complicity within the system. In January 2020, following increased tensions between Iran and the United States in the Persian Gulf, President Trump took the fateful decision to authorize the assassination, by drone attack, of Iran's leading IRGC general, Qasem Soleimani.

Trump had justified this on the basis that he was restoring deterrence, but there was little doubt that the assassination caused deep shock in Iran, most notably in the political leadership. The sense of shock among the wider populace, which had initially led to large demonstrations in sympathy, was however soon overtaken by anger at the accidental shooting down of a Ukrainian airliner flying from Tehran to Kyiv, killing all 176 passengers and crew, including many Canadian Iranian dual citizens. Adulation for Soleimani swiftly turned to anger as crowds began to deface and tear down posters in commemoration of his life.

What this all suggested was a deeper social malaise and anxiety that could flare up at the slightest provocation. Matters were prevented from getting out of hand by the emergence of Covid–19. Iran's vulnerability to Covid was a reflection of its transport ties to China – most obviously Wuhan – the density of its population particularly in the north of the country, and the fact that, like many other governments, the Iranian government failed to take preparatory action. Part of this was a result of not wishing to annoy the Chinese, and indeed Iran had sent a good deal of its PPE supplies to China when the outbreak became apparent.

But what really deterred the government from taking action was its determination, bordering on desperation, to hold a successful parliamentary election that February, and as such it was important to facilitate a high turnout. As it happened, partly because of growing anxieties over Covid but also because of the lacklustre list of candidates, most of whom hailed from the hard-line Principle-ist faction, turnout remained relatively low. But by then the damage had been done.

Initially, the response appeared to be competent, but over time it was clear that the Ministry of Health was taking its lead from the Supreme Leader in almost obsequious terms, accepting his ban on the import of Western-made vaccines and refusing to suspend religious festivals. Quite how many people died as a result of the pandemic will never be known. Statistics were poorly compiled, not least from the provinces, and the way the data was collated differed from that in Western Europe. We do know that the healthcare system was not overwhelmed but it was very badly stretched, and the evidence of excess deaths points to a mortality rate far above the official figures.

By 2021, with Rouhani unable to stand again, the
scene was set for a renewed attempt by Raisi. On this
occasion, little was left to chance, and in the Potemkin
election that followed, in one of the lowest turn-
outs, Raisi became President. He inherited a country
wracked by economic and political discontent, with a
population disenchanted with its ruling class and the
Islamist ideology it promoted. Add to this the resurgence of the Taleban in Afghanistan – which the Raisi
administration welcomed – and the atmosphere had
taken a decidedly grim turn.

Rouhani had attempted in his final months to
re-engage with the new Biden administration on the
JCPOA. But what enthusiasm had existed earlier had
now all but dissipated. Biden had little political capital to spend, and the Iranian Principle-ists, looking
beyond Rouhani, were unwilling for him to have a
parting success. Raisi's new team, meanwhile, were
determined to take their time reviewing the files. With
a complacency born of arrogance, Raisi prolonged the
agony of any return to the JCPOA, insisting on guar-
antees that the Biden administration simply could not
offer. It was only in January 2022 that the negotiations
picked up pace once again.

Domestically, Raisi promised little in terms of
reform, with most viewing him as a technocrat – his
master's voice – but it was an indication of just how
wide the gulf had become between the State and its
society that Raisi's appointment was the cause of much
self-congratulation among the leadership. Covid had

been managed and the presidency was now aligned with the Supreme Leader in a way that would ensure efficient administration and, if need be, a swift succession. The belief that this would be Raisi (rather than the Leader's son Mojtaba) were soon laid to rest by Raisi's mediocre performance as President.

Matters were to come to a head in 2022 with the realization that another crisis might overtake that of Iran and its nuclear programme. With intelligence indicating an imminent Russian invasion of Ukraine, pressure was brought to bear on the Iranians to sign and seal the deal of a resuscitated JCPOA. The Iranians, however, once again misread the runes, believing that a successful Russian invasion would strengthen their own hand. As Russia's attack faltered and sanctions were imposed on the country, Russia then in turn refused to endorse a return to the JCPOA, which would see itself cut off from any potential benefits.

Prospects of agreement receded, and went comatose once Iran decided to throw its weight behind Russia, a decision that reflected ideological symmetries at the expense of national interest. The decision to side with Russia was not entirely unexpected, given the deep bonds which had developed between the political and military leaderships, but it was the intensity of the commitment that took many, not least ordinary Iranians, by surprise. It set the country on a wholly different path.

Meanwhile, on the domestic front, the situation went from bad to worse. The promised dividend from the JCPOA was rapidly receding into the distance, while the economic infrastructure of the country continued to deteriorate through a deleterious absence of investment – amongst the most tragic being the depletion of the country's water resources.

Seemingly oblivious to these underlying strategic tensions, the regime began to impose an especially harsh reading of Islamic Law, especially as it pertained to women's veiling, convinced that only a return to religious purity would ameliorate the country's problems. Such was the brutality of the country's morality police that it was only a matter of time before there was a fatality, and when a Kurdish Iranian woman, Mahsa (Jina) Amini, was tragically killed in custody, the country erupted. The political leadership expressed it was surprised but, if so, it had been blinded to the realities under its feet by its own hubris.

Unlike the two previous protests, this was overtly political and, unlike in 2009, this was not about reform but a fundamental demand for rights. A century after the failure of the Constitutional Revolution, the ideas that had so galvanized Iran were back with a vengeance. Long in gestation, they echoed the ideas born a century earlier and revitalized through a series of protests that could be traced to the Green Movement of 2009. The Islamic Republic had not resolved the myriad crises of its own making. Far from reconciling tradition with modernity, its political and religious leadership had catastrophically exacerbated these tensions and, like its predecessors, it was discovering that you ignore the people at your peril. For the young Iranian women, and men, fighting for their basic rights, it was not so much for ideas whose time had come, but for ones that were long overdue.

Further Reading

An 'essential' history such as this can only highlight some of the major trends, tensions and issues that have defined modern Iranian history, with the hope that it will stimulate the appetite for further reading. Fortunately, the choice for the inquisitive mind is growing, even if the range of material remains relatively limited when compared to what is available for most European countries.

By far the best single-volume history of Iran is by my late colleague and friend Michael Axworthy. His *Iran: Empire of the Mind* (London: Penguin, 2023) is a masterclass in concise erudition, encompassing as he does some 3,000 years of history, interspersing his broad narrative canvas with choice details. His book on *Revolutionary Iran* (London: Penguin, 2023) likewise provides a sound narrative sweep, detailing the causes and consequences of the Islamic Revolution of 1979. Other excellent studies of the modern period include Ervand Abrahamian's *Modern Iran* (Cambridge University Press, 2008), and Saeed Arjomand's *The Turban for the Crown* (Oxford University Press, 1989), a peerless study of the Islamic Revolution which has very much stood the test of time.

Arjomand looks at subsequent developments in his *After Khomeini* (Oxford University Press, 2009). Abbas Amanat's substantive recent tome *Iran: A Modern History* (New Haven: Yale University Press, 2019) looks at the creation of the modern state from 1500 and is especially good on the nineteenth century, while his *Apocalyptic Islam and Iranian Shi'ism* (London: I. B. Tauris, 2009) provides a valuable interrogation of some of the more extreme religious ideas that have permeated Iranian politics. Lastly, in terms of broader histories, there is my own *Modern Iran since 1797* (Abingdon: Routledge, 2019), which also provides some extra detail on the nineteenth-century developments leading to the Constitutional Revolution of 1906.

For the Constitutional Revolution itself, I would recommend three texts, one of which, by the British academic and Persophile Edward Browne, effectively set the narrative template for all subsequent studies. His *Persian Revolution* (Cambridge University Press, 1910) provides a fascinating insight into an unfolding revolution. For Britain's role in first mentoring and then abandoning the movement, Mansour Bonakdarian's comprehensive study of *Britain and the Constitutional Revolution of 1906–11* (New York: Syracuse University Press, 2006) is essential reading. The best collection of articles on the subject is provided by Houchang Chehabi and Vanessa Martin (eds.), *Iran's Constitutional Revolution* (London: I. B. Tauris, 2010).

Details of Reza Shah's rule and the foundations of the modern state can be gleaned from the survey histories noted above, but particular interpretations can also be drawn from Touraj Atabaki and Eric Zurcher's volume on *Men of Order* (London: I. B. Tauris, 2016), and there are useful contributions in Stephanie Cronin's edited volume entitled *The Making of Modern Iran* (Abingdon: Routledge, 2003). For an alternative reading of Reza Shah's role and impact, see my *The Politics of Nationalism in Modern Iran* (Cambridge University Press, 2012).

As we reach the oil nationalization crisis and the coup against Prime Minister Mosaddeq in 1953, matters become more heated and historical accounts increasingly polemical, so readers need to approach texts with this in mind. There are, as one might imagine for this key period, a proliferation of studies. An insightful account is provided by Homa Katouzian, *Musaddiq and the Struggle for Power in Iran* (London: I. B. Tauris, 2009), while useful insights are provided by the Crown Office's recent publication of the official history of the crisis by Rohan Butler, *Britain and the Abadan Crisis, 1950–51* (London: Foreign Office, 2022). For an overview of the period leading to the coup, few can match Fakhreddin Azimi's *Iran: The Crisis of Democracy* (London: I. B. Tauris, 1989).

Moving on to the last Shah, there are fewer book-length studies than one would imagine, with many seeing him simply as a preamble to the Revolution that overthrew him. But significant new work has been provided by Roham Alvandi, *Nixon, Kissinger and the Shah* (Oxford University Press, 2014), which overturns the notion that the Shah was simply an American client, and Robert Steele's recent excellent study of *The Shah's Imperial Celebrations of 1971* (London: I. B. Tauris, 2021), which lays to rest some of the myths about that ill-fated commemoration.

On the particularities of the Islamic Revolution, Siavush Randjbar-Daemi provides a comprehensive account of the history of the presidency in the Islamic Republic in *The Quest for Authority in Iran* (London: I. B. Tauris, 2018). Ervand Abrahamian offers an excellent analysis of the Revolution's debt to the Left in *Khomeinism* (London: I. B. Tauris, 1993). For those interested in my reading of the Islamic Republic's trajectory, my own *Iran, Islam and Democracy: The Politics of Managing Change* (London: Gingko, 2019) is a detailed interpretation of the establishment of the Islamic Republic, through to its emasculation under Ahmadinejad and beyond.

Notes

Introduction: A Revolutionary Land

1 J. Chardin, *A new and accurate description of Persia and other eastern nations*, Vol. II (London, 1724), p. 125.
2 George N. Curzon, *Persia & the Persian Question* (London: Frank Cass, 1966; first published, 1892), Vol. I, pp. 3–4.
3 Ibid., pp. 480–1.

Chapter 1 A Constitutional Revolution (1905–1913)

1 Sir Cecil Spring Rice to Sir Edward Grey, 'General Report on Persia for the Year 1906', reprinted in M. Burrell (ed.), *Iran: Political Diaries 1881–1965* (Chippenham: Archive Editions Ltd, 1997), Vol. III, p. 77. It is worth noting that the senior *mujtahid*, Behbahani, called on the British to support the constitutionalist cause – see M. Bonakdarian, *Britain and the Iranian Constitutional Revolution 1906–1911* (Syracuse University Press, 2006), p. 53.
2 Sir Cecil Spring Rice to Sir Edward Grey, 'General Report on Persia for the Year 1906', p. 75.
3 Sir Arthur Hardinge to Sir Edward Grey, 'General Report on Persia for the Year 1905', reprinted in Burrell (ed.), *Iran: Political Diaries 1881–1965*, pp. 490–4.
4 Sir Cecil Spring Rice to Sir Edward Grey, 'General Report on Persia for the Year 1906', p. 76.
5 Ibid., p. 75.
6 On the role of the 'Russian' Armenians, see Houri Berberian, *Armenians in the Constitutional Revolution of 1905–1911* (Oxford: Westview Press, 2001), p. 226.
7 Sir Cecil Spring Rice to Sir Edward Grey, 'General Report on Persia for the Year 1906', p. 77.

8   For some of these obtuse debates and their rejection by intel-
    lectuals, see H. Bashariyeh, 'Iran and the Critical Passage
    to Democracy', *Aftab Emrooz* 1 Shahrivar 1378 / 23 August
    1999: 7.

9   Sir Cecil Spring Rice to Sir Edward Grey, 'General Report on
    Persia for the Year 1906', p. 77.

10 Ibid., p. 78.

11 Ibid., p. 75.

12 Quoted in Denis Wright, *The English amongst the Persians*
    (London: I. B. Tauris, 1985), p. 30.

13 Mohammad Ali Foroughi, 'The Modernization of Law',
    Journal of Persianate Studies 3 (1), 2010: 31–3.

14 Hasan Taqizadeh, 'Persia's Appeal to England (1908)', in
    Maqalat-e Taqizadeh, Vol. VII (Tehran: Shokufan, 1356/1977),
    p. 453.

15 Taqizadeh, 'Persia's Appeal to England (1908)', p. 462.

16 W. Morgan Shuster, *The Strangling of Persia: Story of the
    European Diplomacy and Oriental Intrigue that Resulted
    in the Denationalization of Twelve Million Mohammedans*
    (Washington: Mage Publishers, 1987; first published 1912),
    pp. 37–8.

17 Ibid., p. xv.

18 R. Ferrier, *The History of the British Petroleum Company*, Vol.
    I: *The Developing Years 1901–32* (Cambridge University Press,
    1982), p. 42.

19 Ibid., p. 60.

Chapter 2 The Rise and Rule of Reza Shah (1914–1940)

1   A good example of this trend is University of Tehran Professor
    Sadeq Zibakalam's recent biography of Reza Shah (2019),
    which paints a highly positive picture of the autocrat nor-
    mally regarded with great antipathy by the intellectual and
    political elite of the Islamic Republic, such that the book had
    to be published in the UK.

2   Ervand Abrahamian, *Tortured Confessions: Prisons and Public
    Recantations in Iran* (Los Angeles: University of California
    Press, 1999), p. 39.

3 Mohammad Ali Jamalzadeh, *Yeki Bud Yeki Nabud* (Berlin: Kavyani, 1340/1960; first published 1922), pp. 110–11.

4 FO 371 18988 E305/305/34, dated 29 December 1934: The National Archive (TNA).

5 M. Roostai, *Tarikh-e nakhostin farhangestan-e iran beh ravayat-e asnad* (Tehran: Nashreney, 1385/2006), p. 83.

6 D. Motadel, 'Iran and the Aryan Myth', in A. M. Ansari (ed.), *Perceptions of Iran: History, Myths and Nationalism from Medieval Persia to the Islamic Republic* (London, I. B. Tauris, 2014), pp. 119–46.

7 FO 371 18992 E4041/608/34, dated 14 June 1935: TNA.

8 FO 371 20048 E3515/405/34, dated 28 May 1936: 'New Dress Regulations': TNA.

9 G. D. Pybus, 'Intelligence Summary No 15 for the Period Ending July 27, 1935', dated 27 July 1935, reprinted in M. Burrell (ed.), *Iran: Political Diaries 1881–1965* (Chippenham: Archive Editions Ltd, 1997), Vol. X, pp. 29–30.

10 Mr Knatchbull-Hugessen to Sir John Simon, E608/608/34, dated 9 January 1935, reprinted in Burrell (ed.), *Iran: Political Diaries 1881–1965*, Vol. X, p. 85.

Chapter 3 Oil and Nationalism (1941–1953)

1 Andrew Roberts, *Churchill: Walking with Destiny* (London: Penguin, 2018), p. 678. See also Ashley Jackson, *Persian Gulf Command: A History of the Second World War in Iran and Iraq* (New Haven: Yale University Press, 2018), p. 150.

2 Jackson, *Persian Gulf Command*, pp. 250–2.

3 See Shaul Bakhash, '"A Matter of Political Expediency": Iran, Britain, South Africa and the Settlement of Reza Shah's Estate', *Middle Eastern Studies* 53 (6), 2017: 986–95.

4 FO 248 1485, 'Persian Govt and Internal Situation' file 21, file nos. 21/44/49, dated 14 February 1949, and 21/36/49, dated 7 February 1949: TNA.

5 *The Times*, 22 June 1949.

6 J. Bamberg, *The History of the British Petroleum Company*, Vol. II: *The Anglo-Iranian Years 1928–1954* (Cambridge University Press, 1994), p. 48.

7 Ibid., p. 50.

8 S. Cronin, 'Popular Politics, the New State and the Birth of the Iranian Working Class: The 1929 Abadan Oil Refinery Strike', *Middle Eastern Studies* 46 (5), September 2010: 705.

9 BP Archive, ArcRef. 43762, 'Report on Delegation to Persia, June 1946', quoted in Touraj Atabaki, 'Chronicle of a Bloody Strike Foretold: Abadan July 1946', in K. H. Roth (ed.), *On the Road to Global Labour History* (Leiden, Boston: Brill, 2017), p. 13.

10 Bamberg, *The History of the British Petroleum Company*, Vol. II, p. 327.

11 Quoted in 'Britain and the Abadan Crisis, 1950–51, Publication of the Official History (1962) by Rohan Butler', *Documents from the British Archives* 5 (FCDO, 2022), p. 46; Bevin's comments are dated 20 July 1946.

12 On these contradictions, see W. Roger Louis, 'American Anti-colonialism and the Dissolution of the British Empire', *International Affairs*, Summer 1985: 395–420.

13 Mostafa Fateh, *Panjah sal naft-e Iran* (Tehran: Payam, 1335/1956), p. 582: speech at the Majles, on 20 Azar 1330 / 12 December 1951.

14 FO 248 1514, 'Internal Situation', summary of Dr Mosaddeq's speech, file no. 10101/368/51, dated 28 September 1951: TNA.

15 FO 371 104561, file 1015, 'Press Reports', file no. 1015/18, dated 28 January 1953: TNA.

16 FO 371 109986 EP 1015/14, 'Political and Economic Situation', dated 12 February 1954: TNA.

4 The 'White' Revolution (1954–1977)

1 FO 248/1569, file 10117, 'Torture in Iran', dated 1956: TNA.

2 FO 371 133055 EP 1671/5, dated 3 October 1958: TNA. Article in *The Spectator*, written by Andrew Roth.

3 Abbas Salvar, interview in *Tarikh-e Mo'aser-e Iran* (Iranian Contemporary History) 1 (4), 1998: 255.

4 Samuel P. Huntington, *Political Order in Changing Societies* (New Haven: Yale University Press, 1968), pp. 6–7.

5 FO 248/1569, Torture in Iran, file 10117/1/56, dated 11 March 1956: TNA.

6 See G. Hambly, 'Attitudes and Aspirations of the Contemporary Iranian Intellectual', *Journal of the Royal Central Asian Society* 51 (2), 1964: 134.

7 For details of the controversy, see the excellent book by R. Steele, *The Shah's Imperial Celebrations of 1971* (London: Routledge, 2020).

8 FCO 96/585, 'Note of the Secretary of State for Energy's Audience with HIM the Shah at Niavaran Palace, Wednesday 7 January 1976 – 11:30 a.m', dated 9 January: TNA.

9 BBC SWB ME/4833/D/1, dated 18 February 1975: Tehran Radio, dated 15 February 1975.

10 BBC SWB ME/4514/D/1, dated 31 January 1974: interview with Peter Snow for ITV, dated 29 January 1974.

5 Revolution and War (1978–1988)

1 Alexis de Tocqueville, *The Old Regime and the Revolution*, Vol. I, ed. F. Furet and F. Melonio, trans. A. S. Kahan (University of Chicago Press, 1998), p. 222.

2 Cyrus Kadivar, 'A Question of Numbers', *Rouzegar-Now* 8 August 2003.

3 Mark Gasiorowski, 'US Intelligence Assistance to Iran, May–October 1979', *Middle East Journal* 66 (4), Autumn 2012: 613–27.

4 See H. W. Beuttel, 'Iranian Casualties in the Iran–Iraq War (1980–1988): A Reappraisal', *The International TNDM Newsletter* 2 (3), December 1997: 6–17. In 2000, INRA reported that official statistics put the total number of deaths at 188,015; quoted in S. Ward, *Immortal: A Military History of Iran and Its Armed Forces* (Washington, DC: Georgetown University Press, 2009), p. 345, fn. 49.

Index